Kommunikation und Kybernetik in Einzeldarstellungen
Herausgegeben von H. Wolter und W. D. Keidel
7

Klaus Weltner

The Measurement of Verbal Information in Psychology and Education

Translated from the German
by Barbara M. Crook

With 82 Figures

Springer-Verlag New York Heidelberg Berlin 1973

Professor Dr. Klaus Weltner
Universität Frankfurt
Institut für Didaktik der Physik

Translation of
Informationstheorie und Erziehungswissenschaft
Verlag Schnelle, Quickborn, 1970

ISBN 0-387-06335-8 Springer-Verlag New York Heidelberg Berlin
ISBN 3-540-06335-8 Springer-Verlag Berlin Heidelberg New York

ISBN 3-87715-054-3 German edition Verlag Schnelle Quickborn

Gratefully dedicated to my father
Ernst Weltner

Preface to the English Edition

Information theory and cybernetics have developed along somewhat different lines in Europe and in the U.S.A. This book is to be seen as a contribution towards bridging the gap.

Anyone who seeks to apply information theory in the fields of education and psychology very soon comes up against a central difficulty: in the form in which it was developed by Shannon information theory excludes the semantic aspect. This problem is fundamental for in education, as in psychology, the semantic aspect is the very heart of the matter. Thus, while Attneave, Miller and Quastler, among others, successfully employed the concepts and units of measurement of information theory in the interpretation of the findings of experimental psychology, they were obliged to restrict their work to its syntactic and statistical aspects.

Before we can make use of the methods and results of information theory in actual teaching, we have to solve the central problem: How can we measure the semantic information of a verbal message? The only way to do this is by extending the theory. A special concept has been developed for this purpose: *subjective information*. In place of an objectively measurable quantity (frequency of sign sequences) we set an empirically determined one: the subjective probability with which the recipient expects a certain sign sequence. The approach is consistent in that we regard subjective information as a function of the recipient and his state of mind at a given time. This is a distinct advance for it enables us to break down subjective information into a semantic part and a syntactic part, using transinformation analysis to isolate the semantic information. Now we can usefully apply the concept of information theory to the problems of educational psychology and teaching.

We can state the information of subject matter to be taught, of rules, definitions and operations, in *bits*, the unit of measurement of information theory. For example, the information of a rule is the semantic information of its redundancy-free formulation in words. Once we can measure the information, we have an index of the complexity of the material.

It is important for teachers to be able to evaluate the subject matter, estimate the extent of the teaching task, and measure the learning increment. Information theory can now be applied for this purpose.

The availability of a uniform theoretical approach offers a number of practical advantages.

The translation of a scientific work is particularly difficult when it deals with a rapidly developing field. The author and his readers thus have reason to be grateful to Mrs. B. M. Crook for her excellent translation, and to Professor H. W. Krohne of Osnabrück University who helped me with the translation of the technical terms.

Frankfurt, May 1973   Klaus Weltner

Preface

The subject matter of this book lies within the scope of the discipline which in recent years has become known as educational cybernetics. We are dealing here with a distinct methodological approach which represents a part of educational cybernetics. However, the term cybernetics has been taken into ordinary usage and is on everyone's lips. Since it may thus be misunderstood, or worse, raise false expectations, we have not used the word cybernetics in the title of this work. Nevertheless, it is necessary to define the position occupied by this approach within the framework of educational cybernetics and its relationship to educational theory in general.

Since Norbert Wiener published his book on cybernetics in 1948, the word cybernetics has been taken to mean a general structural theory centered upon processes which can occur in both living organisms and machines, as well as in social systems. It is based upon the twin concepts of information and feedback. With the development of a quantitative measure for the information conveyed by a communication, a new value—information—joins the fundamental physical values—energy and mass—which form the bedrock of classical technology.

Hermann Schmidt's discourse (1941) on the general significance of feedback marks the founding of the German tradition in cybernetics.

Cybernetics is a "bridge between the sciences" to the extent that it concentrates upon the mathematical representation of structures which are common to many domains. Of necessity, some of its conclusions are formal and general. The public is so much aware of the importance of theoretical or general cybernetics because the development of mathematical models for information processing and exchange has laid the foundations for an advanced technology (by data-processing computer) and the construction of information-processing systems (automation, control of production machinery by process computers).

Cybernetics may be regarded as a subdivision of cybernetics insofar as it deals with the conveying of information in teaching processes, and with the development of mathematical models for learning and teaching systems. At the same time it yields a technique for designing teaching systems in the form of teaching machines and teaching programs. In our modern industrial society, so dependent upon communications, such programs are of increasing significance as an aid to conveying information from teacher to pupil.

In the English-speaking world the unit of information found fairly rapid acceptance in psychological research into processes of perception (Quastler, 1955). Pask (1959) was the first to use the cybernetic approach in the construction of an adaptive teaching machine for training in card punching; this machine adjusted itself to the trainee's learning speed and particular difficulties.

It was not until 1962 that Frank achieved a comprehensive and systematic transference of the cybernetic approach to teaching and learning processes. Frank in building up educational cybernetics used the unit of information developed by Shannon (1949). Von Cube (1965) stressed the concept of redundancy which had been derived from that unit of measurement. These authors' earlier papers go back to 1959. This theoretical and formal approach aroused increasing interest in the questions thus raised—Itelson (1967), Lansky (1967), Landa (1966), Riedel (1964), Weltner (1964). The interest has been further heightened by the scientific and practical work on programs and machines which has gone on since 1964 in the German-speaking countries. In the United States a similar development was based on a behavioral approach (Skinner, 1954), yet the relationship between programmed instruction and educational cybernetics is immediately apparent, since the development of teaching programs and machines is the technical expression of teaching systems. Educational cybernetics is concerned with the description of teaching and learning systems by means of mathematical models.

If we take only the theoretical aspect of educational cybernetics, we see that it comprises on the one hand the basic concept of information with the derived units of measurement: information flow, redundancy, and transinformation, and on the other hand the concept of feedback.

We shall concentrate in this study upon educational processes which can be considered and empirically investigated from the point of view of information exchange and information processing. We shall not deal with the aspects of automata theory or design and construction as they concern educational cybernetics. The object of our research is to develop techniques for the measurement and analysis of the educationally relevant exchange of information.

The unit of information developed by Shannon and Wiener proved inadequate for our purposes because it was conceived as a purely statistical unit of measurement and because the initial concept was of information to be objectively determined by the recipient on the basis of statistical processes. Once the concept of subjective information is introduced, we have to change our notion of the measurement of information, since the value to be measured depends on the internal state of the recipient of the information. This enables the semantic contribution to information to be determined, and this is what is important to educationists. The fundamental concept of information theory—that information is a measure of the novelty value of a message to the recipient—is retained, while the novelty value can be measured by means of expectation probabilities and related to the unit of information. Considerable space will be devoted to the concept of subjective information, to the development and theoretical justification of empirical measuring techniques, and the description of transinformation analysis, since the development of new methods is continually opening up new questions which affect the content of research on educational theory. Hence our work is not to be seen as the endstage of a development, but rather as the unfolding of a methodological concept for which some empirical results are already available and which the author hopes will stimulate further research.

Our work, both theoretical and experimental, has direct relevance for three areas:

a) The general theory of teaching, because the observance of the fundamental limitations which exist for any exchange of information, and the possibility of defining the didactic information of the subject be taught, enable us to make quantitative statements about the level of difficulty of the subject matter. This again enables us to set limits for teaching targets in the processes of teaching and learning. In practice, this program takes us as far as establishing units of teaching which are tolerable for children. It is possible to demonstrate by analyzing the flow of information during teaching that excessive demands are placed upon the pupil when the subjective information flow exceeds certain values, and that this induces a decline in learning performance. Excessive demands upon the teaching system—the teacher—occur when he is required to consider every message that comes back to him from the pupils, since the flow of information to be processed by the teacher will then exceed the given limits.

b) The theory of educational objectives and the analysis of thought processes. If educational concepts are to describe the development of interactions between persons and their environment, such interactions must also be regarded as communication in the sense of information theory. The analysis of forms of communication and of information processing leads us straight to the complex problems associated with thought processes and thought forms. Thus we can obtain from information theory criteria for the selection of educational objectives and the attainment of optimal mental attitudes.

c) The social aspect of educational systems. The child's ability to communicate in words is an essential requirement for his socialization and scholastic success. In the meantime, sociological research has made a start by analyzing speech behavior as a determinant in educational processes and social selection mechanisms. Analysis by means of information theory of the subjectively available speech repertory may contribute to the elucidation of the role played by "formal languages" and "public languages". "Formal languages" should have a high degree of informational efficiency, whereas "public languages" because of their stereotyped, behavior-related speech patterns might be expected to show higher pragmatic effectiveness.

I cordially thank, for their assistance and support in carrying out the empirical research, the Lehramtskandidaten A. Braun, Ch. Böttcher, F. Menke, E. Rachut, W. Röhrig, G. Wolff and K. Warnkross, also Stud. Ass. P.-B. Heinrich, Realschullehrer W. Kunze and päd. Ass. R. Zorn. The work was financially supported by the Volkswagen Foundation.

Table of Contents

1 Foundations of Information Theory

1.1 The Communication System

1.1.1 Introduction

In its original form, information theory refers to exchanges of signals between technical systems. When its concepts and methods are applied to human communication processes and these are studied in the light of and by the methods of information theory, it is necessary at first to disregard the complex character of the possible forms of communication. This, of course, exposes us to the criticism that the relationships investigated are irrelevant. Weaver, who wrote an introduction to Shannon's (1949) fundamental work on information theory, appreciated and discussed this difficulty. He distinguished three levels at which the exchange of information takes place:

A) the statistical level;

B) the semantic level;
this involves the question: When signals are sent, does the recipient receive and decode the signals correctly so as to understand their meaning?

C) the pragmatic level;
here the question is: When a message has been received, does the recipient change his behavior in the way intended by the sender?

Mathematical information theory makes statements at level A) and so, Weaver argues, the laws governing this formal exchange of information provide the basis for an understanding of the process of communication at levels B) and C).

What interests the educational theorist is the multiplicity of interactions between human beings. He is interested exclusively in levels B) and C). Nevertheless, it is a fascinating thought that the complex interaction involved in human communication might be traced back through a sequence, however long, of intermediate steps to an origin determined by the mathematical unit of information.

In physics, the fundamental concept of energy defines the framework ordering and bounding physical relationships; yet a knowledge of the law of conservation of energy, for example, does not enable us correctly to derive principles for the design and construction of machines or energy transducers. In the same way, a knowledge of the aspects of communication processes which can be described in terms of information theory can determine the framework within which complex communications may be classified and understood.

The rules, conditions, and laws which can be expected from the application of the procedures of information theory to education often have the character of necessary but not sufficient conditions. Thus, a knowledge of these laws is no substitute for creative imagination and ingenuity in teaching, any more than a knowledge of the main laws of thermodynamics is a substitute for the constructive imagination of the engineer in developing thermodynamic machinery.

We cannot expect to derive an instruction book for teachers directly from the application of the methods of information theory. We do, however, derive procedures which can help us to analyze the communication processes relevant to teaching and to test the feasibility of any plan of action.

1.1.2   The Basic Problems of Information Theory

In the area of human communications, and this includes communications between teacher and pupil, it is possible to distinguish cases at different levels of complexity.

The simplest case is that of directional, one-way communication, where information flows from one partner to the other. This simple scheme may be realized in many ways. It may be communication between one teacher and one pupil, or conversely communication of one pupil with one teacher. This scheme is realized in pure form in a radio talk, in television, or the cinema.

In these examples the role of one partner is characterized by his passivity and assimilation of information during the communication, while the other partner is actively generating information. Meyer-Eppler

Fig. 1.1   Directional, one-way communication between two partners S_1 and S_2 — radio talk, television, film, and as an approximation, also lecture.

Fig. 1.2   Two-way communication between two partners (people or technical systems) — discussion, communication between adaptive teaching machine and pupil.

(1959) calls this "living" information. In a figurative sense communication between a book and a person also falls into this category. Meyer-Eppler calls this "dead" information because it is stored in a data bank and requires activation by the communication partner.

The next higher step is two-way communication with the two partners exchanging information. This is realized in conversations between teacher and pupil, conversations between two persons in general, and communication between a pupil and a teaching machine where the behavior of the adaptive teaching machine depends upon the pupil's reactions. In this case we are dealing with a feedback cycle.

The scheme reaches a higher degree of complexity when more than two communication partners are involved. Fig. 1.3 shows in diagram

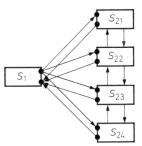

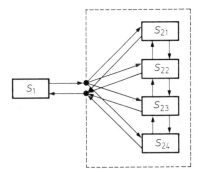

Fig. 1.3 Communication between one partner S_1 and many other partners, who may also communicate amongst themselves. Teacher–pupils in a class.

Fig. 1.4 Simplified communication scheme.

form the communication between one teacher and four pupils, who may also communicate amongst themselves. Within this complex scheme, if we select a given aspect, for example, communication from teacher to pupils, we can recognize the simple cases. The pupils can be considered collectively as a complex integrated system and the teacher may be considered to communicate with this system (see Fig. 1.4). Even though the situation has been formally simplified and we have in principle derived the second scheme, we must not forget that the arrow stands for an information flow of any level of complexity. What has been said here about the communication partners applies equally to the various possible channels of communication, such as speech, writing, gestures, and mime.

The first step in applying theory is to investigate and analyze the information flow and to ask how much of this information flow can be measured. Later on we shall be interested in the way in which the communication partners process the information.

1.1.3   The Simple Communication System

A consideration of the model of one-way communication between partners reveals a whole range of possible realizations. In addition to direct communication, one may also consider communication via technical intermediates. The next diagram (Fig. 1.5) shows Meyer-Eppler's version of a verbal communication system.

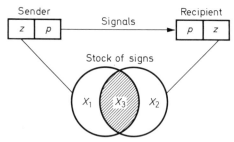

Fig. 1.5   Communication scheme according to Meyer-Eppler. p=peripheral organs; z=central (conscious) organs; x_1=sender's active stock of signs; x_2=recipient's passive stock of signs; x_3=common stock of signs.

The message is generated by the sender and is received by the percipient. In information theory the terms used are transmitter and receiver, respectively. The signs used for the transmission of information are taken from a repertory of signs common to both partners. Information theory does, of course, postulate the existence of a repertory of signs common to both partners, but let us point out at this stage that one of the fundamental problems of education and part of the socialization of an adolescent is to build up the knowledge of that sign repertory common to his culture. One of the most important teaching processes is to enlarge the sign repertory common to teacher and pupil. The distinction made in Fig. 1.5 between the central and peripheral organs already allows for the fact that, when two conscient beings communicate by means of the peripheral organs, the tools of hearing and speech—one might almost call them technical intermediates—are necessary before information exchange is even possible.

The communication system may now be extended by technical transmission links such as the telephone. It would seem as if in principle nothing new has been added: Fig. 1.6 shows an extension in the form of a transmitter (microphone), a transmission line, and a receiver (loudspeaker). Interfering signals (noise) may arise during transmission from transmitter to receiver and make it difficult for the receiver to recognize the signals.

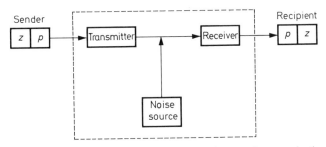

Fig. 1.6   Technical communication system as an element of communication.

This is accounted for by inserting a noise source, so that the signal at the receiver does not completely correspond to the signal emitted from the transmitter. Now the subject matter of mathematical information theory is that part of the communication system which consists of the transmitter, the receiver, and the noise source. It is to this restricted technical system that the concepts and theorems of information theory apply.

Educational theory, where the interest lies exclusively in the communication between sender and percipient, is therefore faced with the question whether the methods and concepts developed by information theory will be found to have any relevance for the complete communication system. All technical systems are used to assist communication between sender and percipient. Any improvement in the technical aids merely serves to improve communication between the first and last links in the system.

In this chapter the basic concepts of information theory and its associated problems will first be developed. It will then be shown that the basic concept of information theory, the unit of information, can be applied to the entire communication system. This has already led to the development of practical procedures, and these are described and explained individually. This work goes beyond the scope of mathematical information theory in that it extends the statistical approach by introducing the mental state of the recipient. In the process, some of the axiomatic assumptions of information theory, such as the ergodicity of the source, are abandoned. The center of attention then becomes the way in which the information received depends upon the state of mind of the recipient at the time of receipt.

The procedure of transinformational analysis next opens up the semantic level (B). This enables aspects of the learning process, the transmission of information during teaching, and other phenomena relevant to educational theory to be quantified.

Finally, we shall be in a position to draw conclusions concerning a theory of teaching, deducing from our unitary approach rules and limits for educational procedures.

1.2 Concepts of Information Theory

First, the basic concepts of information theory will be developed as far as is necessary for an understanding of the later sections and its applications in education.

1.2.1 Information

1.2.1.1 Signs, Repertory, Alphabet

Information theory is based on the scheme of the communication system. Its observations are restricted to the technology of communication, namely, transmitter, transmission channel, noise source, and receiver. Messages are transmitted as a sequence of signs. The signs are associated with physically measurable phenomena, the signals. The signals are electrical impulses, sound waves, light signals, black marks on paper having a definite shape and which we recognize as letters, changes in the amplitude or frequency of electrical waves, and so on. The signal only becomes a sign when it is given a meaning. The meanings assigned to the signals must be agreed between sender and recipient; they then become signs and systems of signs, like letters, words in a language, technical symbols, mathematical symbols, or pictures.

Communication presupposes the use of only such signs as are known to both sender and recipient.

The set of all distinguishable signs x_j in a stock of signs is called the repertory R. Their number r is called the potency of the repertory R. The different signs of a repertory are called the alphabet. For messages consisting of letter sequences, the term alphabet means the same as it does in ordinary language.

In information theory the concept of the alphabet is refined and may be assigned to any system of signs or events. The refinement is that in information theory an alphabet is always assumed to be closed and bounded.

The assignment consists in applying the idea of an alphabet to such general events as the outcome of a football match, the results of physical experiments, grades for school work, attitudes of teachers, the Morse code, flag signals, etc. The alphabet of a repertory is then the defined set of all possible events. Thus, information theory does not apply only to messages about events, it also assigns the same treatment to the sources of the messages, that is, to the events themselves.

The assumption of a finite alphabet represents an idealization which is permissible and is fulfilled in practice for technical information transmission systems.

Such phenomena as processes of communication between people, or the perception of events in the external world, where the percipient is a human being, can only be considered an approximation to the process of information reception with a closed repertory. A human being always puts signs into an open repertory because he is always—though often with very low probability—expecting events which are not predictable with reference to the existing repertory of perception. Thus it may happen that a teacher will talk about a political event during a mathematics lesson. Unforeseen events bring about a change in the repertory of perception.

Example. Fire may break out while a film is being shown. The repertory of perception is shifted from apperception of the film to the search for escape.

Though the probability of these and similar events is very small, it is different from zero, and human beings are always attuned to it.

1.2.1.2 Frequency, Probability, Field

The elements of a repertory have a certain probability of occurrence which may be determined statistically by counting the frequency of the individual elements in a rather large random sample of messages. For large random samples, the relative frequency moves towards the probability of occurrence with any desired degree of accuracy. The relative frequency of a sign x_j is

$$h_j = \frac{N_j}{N} \qquad (1\text{--}1)$$

if the sign occurs N_j times and there is a total of N characters.

Thus the recipient of the sequence of signs can calculate the frequency of occurrence because

$$h_j \to p_j \quad \text{when} \quad N \to \infty.$$

This relation holds only so long as the source of the signs can be considered an ergodic source. In ergodic sources, by definition, the frequency distribution of their signs is constant. With this assumption, the location of the random sample in the sign sequence is a matter of indifference.

A repertory in which the probability of occurrence of each individual element is defined is called a field or schema.

1.2.1.3   Information and Probability of Expectation

The more unexpected an event or a sign, the greater is its information. Its information approaches zero when the receiver can expect the sign with certainty. In the restricted sense of information theory, information is a measure of the novelty value of the sign for the receiver. One may also consider information as a measure of the uncertainty of a situation, which will be removed by the occurrence of an event from the field of possible events.

Thus, the unit of information is related to those components of the meaning of the term information in ordinary language that relate to novelty or rarity.

The information of a message has nothing to do with its importance for the recipient. Take these two messages:

"You have won the first prize" and

"There is a hedgehog in the garden".

They may contain equal information, but the former is likely to be deemed much more important by the recipient.

The following examples will clarify and define our considerations:

A. The information source is a random process having two events.

Let the source of information be the result of a series of coin tossings. Whether the coin comes down heads or tails, this is a concrete example of an ergodic information source. If the results of a series of tosses are transmitted one after the other by means of a technical communication system, two sorts of signs will be required for their transmission. The relationship between the original information, heads or tails, and the transmitted signal, dot or dash, positive or negative impulse, is quite clear. The fact that a definite signal is assigned to the result of the toss makes this signal into a sign.

The uncertainty at the receiving end concerning each new message may be stated by means of probability theory. With a completely symmetrical coin, both results, heads or tails, are equally likely. Both have the probability $p=0.5$. This probability may be determined empirically by recording the frequency of occurrence of heads and tails for a very large number of tosses. The relative proportion of both events will approach 0.5.

$$h_{heads}=\frac{N_{heads}}{N} \xrightarrow[N \to \infty]{} p_{heads}=0.5. \tag{1-2}$$

We get the same result if we consider instead of the information source the sign sequence in the transmission system.

B. The information source is a random process having all events equally probable.

Let the information source be a drum. Let the drum contain slips of paper with the letters A to Z and with signs for word spacer, period, comma, semicolon, hyphen, and question mark. The drum contains an equal number of each sign. Slips are drawn and then put back into the drum, so that the number of slips remains the same. As the slips are drawn in succession, a sequence of signs is obtained which may be transmitted by technical signals. These sequences have little resemblance to ordinary texts. It is precisely this difference which we will be investigating later on.

For the recipient, the uncertainty concerning a character in the continuing sequence has increased. The probability that a definite sign x_j will occur is $p_j = \frac{1}{32}$.

This probability, too, can be empirically determined by recording the relative frequency of each individual sign in a large random sample.

The result will be the same, whether we consider the technically transmitted sign sequence or the sequence of events at the actual information source. If a recipient tries to predict the next sign, he will be successful in half of all cases for coin tossing. When predicting letters, etc., his guesses will be correct on average once every 32 signs. The information of the signs in the second example increases as the probability p_j of the event decreases. Shannon (1949) and Wiener (1948) put forward the relation

$$i(x_j) = \operatorname{ld} \frac{1}{p_j} \qquad\qquad (1\text{--}3)$$

as a measure of the information i of sign x_j. ld is the abbreviation for "logarithmus dualis", that is, the logarithm to base 2; see Fig. 1.7. Following a suggestion by Tukey, the unit of measurement for information is called a "bit"; this is an abbreviation of "binary digit".

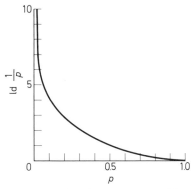

Fig. 1.7   Information of an element or event with probability p.

In coin tossing, each event has the information

$$i(x_{\text{heads}}) = i(x_{\text{tails}}) = \text{ld}\,\frac{1}{0.5} = \text{ld}\,2 = 1 \text{ bit.}$$

The slips in the drum have more information:

$$i(x_j) = \text{ld}\,\frac{1}{p_j} = \text{ld}\,\frac{1}{\frac{1}{32}} = \text{ld}\,32 = \text{ld}\,2^5 = 5 \text{ bits.}$$

In general, for a repertory of r equally probable signs

$$i(x_j) = \text{ld}\,\frac{1}{p_j} = \text{ld}\,\frac{1}{\frac{1}{r}} = \text{ld}\,r. \tag{1-4}$$

The function $i = \text{ld}\,r$ is shown in Fig. 1.8.

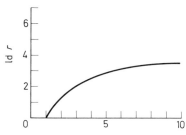

Fig. 1.8   Information of equally likely elements of a repertory of magnitude r.

C. The information source is a random process having all events not equally probable. Instead of a coin, we toss a cigarette pack. The events are of three kinds:

1) Case (x_1): the pack lies on one of its large faces.
2) Case (x_2): the pack lies on one of its medium-sized faces.
3) Case (x_3): the pack lies on one of its small faces.

The sequence of results is transmitted over a communication system. All three events do not have equal probability. The pack will generally fall on one of its large faces and will seldom stand on end. The probability of each of the three events may be empirically determined by calculating the relative frequency of each individual event. If the probabilities are p_j, then

$$\sum_{1}^{3} p_j = 1. \tag{1-5}$$

When the pack stands on end, this event has the greatest information value for the recipient. The measure of information is applied to events of unequal probability

$$i(x_j) = \operatorname{ld} \frac{1}{p_j}. \qquad (1\text{--}6)$$

Let us assume the recipient of the sequence of messages has counted the frequency of the three events and has found:

$$p_1 = 0.80,$$
$$p_2 = 0.18,$$
$$p_3 = 0.02.$$

In this case the field of events X is given by the schema

$$\begin{pmatrix} x_1 & x_2 & x_3 \\ 0.80 & 0.18 & 0.02. \end{pmatrix}$$

Therefore the information of the three events is (see 5.5 for a table of the functions ld $1/p$):

$$i(x_1) = 0.322 \text{ bit},$$
$$i(x_2) = 2.474 \text{ bits},$$
$$i(x_3) = 5.644 \text{ bits}.$$

Besides the information of the individual events, one may also determine their average information. This is not the same as the average value of the information of the elements. We must allow for the fact that the relative frequency of the events differs, so that the frequently occurring events by that very fact contribute more to the average value of information. If we form a weighted mean, we obtain directly the mean information of the events of a field X (Shannon, 1949). The contribution of sign x_j to the mean value is then $p_j \operatorname{ld} \dfrac{1}{p_j}$; see Fig. 1.9

$$H(X) = \sum_1^r p_j \operatorname{ld} \frac{1}{p_j}. \qquad (1\text{--}7)$$

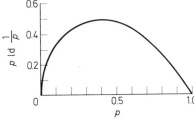

Fig. 1.9 Contribution of an element or event having probability p to the average information of the field, or sequence of events.

In our example,

$$H_{\text{pack}} = \sum_1^3 p_j \operatorname{ld} \frac{1}{p_j} = 0.257 + 0.445 + 0.113 = 0.815 \; bits.$$

The average information or entropy H describes the uncertainty prior to the occurrence of any event from field X. The information of the event when it has actually occurred may deviate upwards or downwards. So, in our example, when the most frequent case occurs and the cigarette pack falls on its large face, the information lies below the average value. The information of the pack standing upright on its small face lies appreciably above the average value.

The average value $H(X)$ of the information of a field describes both the average information of the signs of a sequence and the uncertainty concerning an event from field X prior to its occurrence. For the sake of brevity, we say that $H(X)$ describes the uncertainty of field X.

If we make our cigarette pack into a cube, all three events become equally probable. Then the information becomes

$$i(x_1) = i(x_2) = i(x_3) = \operatorname{ld} 3 = 1.586$$
$$H_{\text{cube}} = \operatorname{ld} 3 = 1.586.$$

Comparison with H_{pack} shows that the average information decreases when all events are not equally probable. One of the fundamental theorems of information theory states that for a field X with r elements

$$H(X) \leq \operatorname{ld} r. \tag{1-8}$$

The equals sign applies for equal probabilities of all elements (for proof, see Jaglom, 1956).

D. The information source is a random process.

We may use the approach of information theory to consider far less simple events than the examples from probability theory. Let the repertory of possible events be visitors standing at our apartment door and ringing the bell. For each possible visitor there is a probability of expectation p_j such that

$$\sum_1^r p_j = 1. \tag{1-9}$$

If a neighbor rings the bell, the information is less than if it were a school friend living in a distant city who has not visited us for a long time. Here too, the average information is

$$H(X)=\sum_{1}^{r} p_j \operatorname{ld} \frac{1}{p_j}.$$

However, the probabilities of expectation p_j corresponding to the particular situation of the recipient have still to be inserted. The repertory of possible visitors is open, since all persons alive at the time must be considered as potential visitors, even though for the vast majority the probability of expectation is virtually zero. If the computation is carried out for a limited r, that is, for a closed repertory, then too low a value of $H(X)$ is obtained, but the systematic error can be estimated and determined within limits.

1.2.2 Coding, Binary Coding, Supersigns

We understand by coding a ruling according to which the signs of a repertory X are unmistakably assigned to the signs of another repertory Y. However, the number of elements in repertories X and Y may be different. The signs of repertory Y may be of a composite kind, so that a sequence of signs from Y may represent one sign from repertory X. We then say that the X sign is represented by a code word from repertory Y. Examples of coding are the assignment of letters to Morse signals, of sounds to letters, etc.

An extreme case, but one of great practical significance, is the coding of any repertory by another which contains only two elements. These may be 1 and 0, L and O, + and $-$. Such signs are technically easy to produce by means of such signals as "current on" or "current off", "magnetize" or "demagnetize". Clearly, in this case the code words will be rather long if the initial repertory X is larger than 2. This kind of coding is called binary coding. In binary coding, the length of the code word depends on the number r of elements from field X to be coded.

If X contains two elements, the code word length will be 1.

If X contains four elements, the code word length will be 2, since there are only four different ways of combining two signs:

$$x_1 = LL$$
$$x_2 = LO$$
$$x_3 = OL$$
$$x_4 = OO$$

If X contains eight elements, the code word length will be 3. In general, the code word length l will be:

$$l = \mathrm{ld}\, r; \text{ when } r = 2^n, \text{ then}$$
$$l = \mathrm{ld}\, 2^n = n.$$

In this case the code word length l is the same as the information i from 2^n equally probable events x_j:

$$i(x_j) = \mathrm{ld}\, \frac{1}{\left(\frac{1}{2^n}\right)} = \mathrm{ld}\, 2^n = n. \tag{1-10}$$

The equation also applies to sign sequences which occur with different relative frequencies.

Shannon's formula here yields an average information which is smaller than the average information where the distribution is uniform. If we desire a code where the length of the composite messages will be as short as possible, then signs which occur frequently can be assigned short code words, longer code words being given to signs which occur less frequently. Methods for constructing such codes were given by Huffman (1952).

If the relative frequencies of the signs can be stated in the form $\frac{1}{2^n}$, then the code word length will be $l = n$. For optimal coding, therefore, the code word length of a sign will coincide with the information of that sign, so that the information of a sign may also be understood as its code word length under optimal coding. On this assumption the mean code word length of the signs of field X is identical with the average information $H(X)$ or entropy of the field.

If the relative frequencies of the elements of field X cannot be represented by $p_j = \frac{1}{2^n}$, then the average information $H(X)$ denotes the lower limit of the average code word length; the lower limit may be approximated by optimal coding (Huffman, 1952).

Supersigns. Signs may be combined into sign complexes which in turn may be viewed as independent units of a new repertory. Following Frank (1959), we shall call such sign complexes supersigns.

The words of written language are such supersigns in relation to the sequence of letters. Words are independent elements in both optical and acoustical perception. Sentences represent the next larger sign complex. Here, too, there are stereotyped forms that may be considered as supersigns. A supersign hierarchy is built up in the transitions from letters to words, from words to sentences, and in some cases from sentences to larger logical systems. Within the hierarchy, a given sign may be a supersign relative to a subsign, and it may itself be a subsign in relation to a higher sign repertory. In describing processes of communication or perception, it is always necessary to indicate the supersign repertory within which perception takes place.

The letters of the alphabet can form words in the German and Latin languages as well as in English. There are other possible letter combinations that do not correspond to any word in any language. The supersign repertory of English words is smaller than the repertory of possible letter combinations. When the number of supersigns is smaller than the number of possible combinations of the subsigns, information decreases when perception takes place in the supersign repertory.

Formation of supersigns via complex formation: The formation of supersigns by combining sign lattices or sign complexes into new units is not restricted to the formation of spoken or written supersigns. At the level of perception, diverse perceived elements are already combined into new units. The complex "house" contains elements such as doors, windows, walls, roof, chimney. The supersign "automobile" contains such heterogeneous elements as wheels, lights, seats, windshield, doors, and so on.

If the elements of a supersign created by complex formation are independent of each other, the probability of occurrence of the supersign is equal to the product of the probability of occurrence of each individual element. But if, on the other hand, there are relationships between the individual elements, say, of a functional nature, as in the example of the automobile, then the probability of occurrence of the complex is greater than the product of the probabilities of occurrence of the individual elements. Thus the supersign will have less information than the sum of the information of the elements.

Formation of supersigns via category formation: The letter A may be coded according to typeface by series of different signs: **a, A** (boldface); *a, A* (italic); a, A (roman); ɑ, 𝔄 (Gothic). But these different symbols for the letter A will not be perceived by the reader as being different symbols, rather they will be read as A independently of the typeface. The supersign A, which arose from category formation and which may be represented by a repertory of different signs, has less information than each individual sign. Some of the difficulties inherent in automatic character recognition are due to the fact that, while human beings will readily form supersigns from letters via category formation despite quite considerable differences between the various typefaces and alphabets, such problems are not so easily solved by technical means. Supersign formation via category formation is only feasible for structured signs. In forming supersigns, a distinction is made between the relevant and irrelevant features of a sign.

Formation of supersigns via category formation is what an automobile driver does in heavy traffic: he sees merely automobiles, bicycles, pedestrians and trucks, and ignores the differences within each category. Supersigns of higher order can arise simultaneously when they are formed via both complex and category formation.

The supersign control system is a complex with respect to its elements and their interrelationships: controlled variable, adjusting element, control object, control error, reference component. The supersign "control system" is a category relative to the various forms in which it occurs in biology, technology, cybernetics, economics, and education.

1.2.3   The Product Field

One can consider two or more fields together and combine them into a product field. All imaginable combinations of events from the fields X and Y are considered as new elements in the product field. The number of elements of the product field is greater than those of the separate fields, and is equal to the product of the number r_1 of elements from field X and the number r_2 of elements from field Y. The elements of a product field are best shown in a matrix.

An obvious example of two independent fields is provided by the field of coin tossing and by the field of a pupil's grade for a mathematics exercise. There is a total of twelve possible combinations of the two results of a coin toss and the six possible, though not equally probable, marks for the exercise. The probabilities of expectation for the twelve elements of the product field are defined by the probabilities of the original fields.

The information of an element $x_j y_k$ of the product field XY is therefore given by

$$i(x_j y_k) = \operatorname{ld} \frac{1}{p(x_j y_k)}. \qquad (1\text{--}11)$$

toss	mark					
	1	2	3	4	5	6
heads	H1	H2	H3	H4	H5	H6
	p_{h1}	p_{h2}	p_{h3}	p_{h4}	p_{h5}	p_{h6}
tails	T1	T2	T3	T4	T5	T6
	p_{t1}	p_{t2}	p_{t3}	p_{t4}	p_{t5}	p_{t6}

If, as in this example, the fields X and Y are independent of each other, then

$$p(x_j y_k) = p(x_j) \cdot p(y_k) \tag{1-12}$$

so that

$$i(x_j y_k) = \operatorname{ld} \frac{1}{p(x_j) \cdot p(y_k)} = \operatorname{ld} \frac{1}{p(x_j)} + \operatorname{ld} \frac{1}{p(y_k)} = i(x_j) + i(y_k). \tag{1-13}$$

The information of the elements of the product field is equal to the sum of the information of the individual events. The mean information of the product field of independent fields is equal to the sum of the mean information of the original fields

$$H(XY) = \sum_j \sum_k p(x_j y_k) \cdot \operatorname{ld} \frac{1}{p(x_j y_k)}$$

$$= \sum_j \sum_k p(x_j) \cdot p(y_k) \left(\operatorname{ld} \frac{1}{p(x_j)} + \operatorname{ld} \frac{1}{p(y_k)} \right)$$

$$= \sum_j p(x_j) \operatorname{ld} \frac{1}{p(x_j)} + \sum_j p(x_j) H(Y) \tag{1-14}$$

$$H(XY) = H(X) + H(Y). \tag{1-15}$$

1.2.4 Conditional Probability

So far, we have assumed that the signs in a sign sequence (coin tosses, or slips drawn from a drum) or the events in a sequence of events (visitors) are independent of one another. We have combined such fields into product fields. However, they are not as a rule independent. Fields may be more or less dependent on one another. One limiting value is complete independence, the other is total dependence and there are any number of transitional states between these two limits. We say two events are stochastically dependent when the occurrence of the first event changes the probability of occurrence of the second.
Example.
First Event. The bell rings. Olaf, a neighbor's boy, comes to watch television.
Second Event. The bell rings. Olaf's visit has changed the field of possible visitors. We are not particularly friendly with Olaf's mother, and she rarely

calls on us. However, since Olaf is with us, the probability that his mother will come to fetch him has increased.

If we consider stochastically dependent events in general, then these may be:

1. Events from two stochastically dependent fields X and Y;
example. field X: showers; field Y: cloudiness.

2. Stochastically interdependent elements from sequences of events or signs;

example. sequences of letters, words, or visitors. The probability that event y_k from field Y will occur once we know that event x_j of field X has occurred is called conditional probability. We write it as

$$p(y_k|x_j).$$

For product fields with stochastic dependence,

$$H(XY) \leq H(X) + H(Y). \tag{1-16}$$

If we write $H(Y|X)$ to denote the information of field Y when field X is known, we further obtain

$$H(XY) = H(X) + H(Y|X) \tag{1-17}$$

and

$$H(XY) = H(Y) + H(X|Y). \tag{1-18}$$

Then for the conditional information of field Y with the assumption that X is known, we have

$$H(Y|X) \leq H(Y). \tag{1-19}$$

If we know field X on which field Y depends stochastically, then the mean information of field Y is reduced. Our knowledge can only decrease the information of Y; for proofs, see Frank (1969) and Jaglom (1967).

Stochastic dependence frequently occurs among successive signs in sign sequences. The conditional information is determined for bigrammatic dependence by taking into account the preceding sign, for trigrammatic dependence the two preceding signs, and for n-grammatic dependence the n preceding signs.

1.2.5 Transinformation

The concept of information theory which is central to the problems posed in education is transinformation. The transinformation of a field

X onto a field Y, or the transinformation of a single event x_j onto a field X or an event y_k, is the expression of the information which the knowledge of one field contributes to another. In other words, one field already contains some information concerning the other. The average information of the product field where there is stochastic dependence is smaller than the sum of the average information of the original fields,

$$H(XY) \leq H(X) + H(Y).$$

The difference between the information of the product field for stochastic dependence and for independence is the transinformation $T(XY)$ of either field into the other. The transinformation therefore is a measure of the field interdependence—resembling the correlation factor in statistics; see Attneave (1959) and Kullback (1959).

The relationship which exists between the mean information of field X and that of field Y, as well as between the mean information of a product field and the conditional information, is shown in the figure below. It is assumed here that both fields are stochastically interdependent. Then transinformation takes place from one field into the other. The equations expressing these relations may be read off directly from the figure (see Quastler, 1955).

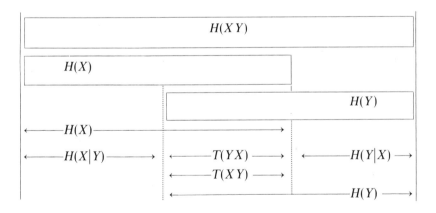

$$T(XY) = H(X) + H(Y) - H(XY) \qquad (1\text{–}20)$$

$$T(YX) = H(Y) + H(X) - H(XY). \qquad (1\text{–}21)$$

The transinformation of field X into field Y is equal to the transinformation of field Y into field X. The transinformation is a symmetrical relationship, exactly the same information about Y being contained in field X as information about X in field Y.

$$T(XY) = H(X) - H(X|Y)$$
$$T(XY) = H(Y) - H(Y|X).$$

(1–22)

Transinformation in this form is expressed by the difference between the information of field X with and without knowledge of field Y (conditional information). Transinformation analysis, which will be applied to practical problems in Chapter 3, is based on these relationships. The values of $H(X)$ and $H(X|Y)$ may be empirically determined in many cases. Finally, it is also true that

$$H(XY) = H(X) + H(Y) - T(XY).$$

(1–23)

What has been said here concerning mean information may also be applied to the determination of the information of individual events. In this case, the mean information H is replaced by the information of the individual event x_j. The transinformation of event x_j into event y_k is then

$$T(x_j, y_k) = i(y_k) - i(y_k|x_j).$$

(1–24)

The example also illustrates the two limiting cases, i.e. the existence of complete independence or complete dependence between the two fields. In the first case transinformation vanishes; in the second case, the fields X and Y are clearly transformable one into the other, one field coding for the other. In this case the transinformation becomes equal to the information of the two individual fields.

1.2.6   Redundancy

The information of a field attains its highest value when all events or elements are equally probable. When the different probabilities assigned to the individual elements are taken into consideration, the mean information declines. If one further considers the existence of stochastic dependences between individual elements, the information declines still further. The concept of redundancy allows us to describe the relative proportion by which the actual information remains below the maximum information. We know that with optimal coding the code word length is proportional to the information; therefore redundancy is also a measure of the extent to which a message can be shortened by using an optimal code. Taking the frequency distribution into account, the value for redundancy is given by

$$R = \frac{H_0 - H_1}{H_0} \qquad (1\text{-}25)$$

where H_0 is the maximum information of the field and H_1 is the information when the frequency distribution is taken into account. The redundancy value always refers to two states, which have to be defined. In our case H_0 expresses the state where all events of a field are equally probable, and H_1 the state which takes into account the information decline due to the known frequency distribution. If, in general, we take into account the dependence of consecutive events (bigrammatic or n-grammatic dependence), then we obtain for the conditional information H_n

$$R = \frac{H_0 - H_n}{H_0}. \qquad (1\text{-}26)$$

It is clear from this that the redundancy value must always be qualified by stating the initial condition H_0 and the dependences in H.

Redundancy of Supersigns. If a sign sequence from a supersign repertory is being perceived, its information for the formation of supersigns via categories will always be less than in the subsign repertory, whereas, for the formation of supersigns via complexes, it will be less on average.

The redundancy of the sign sequence

$$R = \frac{I\,(\text{subsign sequence}) - I\,(\text{supersign sequence})}{I\,(\text{subsign sequence})} \qquad (1\text{-}27)$$

or

$$R = 1 - \frac{I\,(\text{supersign sequence})}{I\,(\text{subsign})} \qquad (1\text{-}28)$$

was called supersign redundancy by Cube (1960).

1.2.6.1 *Information Flow Rate, Channel Capacity*

If information is transmitted via a technical channel, the information flow rate may be determined as information transmitted per unit of time. The information flow rate is given in bits/sec. The capacity of a technical transmission channel sets the upper limit for the information flow that can be transmitted per unit of time via the channel. The concept of information flow rate and of transmission limits set by predetermined channel capacities may be applied directly to communication between people, and to processes of learning and perception.

1.2.6.2 Noise, Interfering Source

Interference occurs during the transmission of messages over technical systems, and this is known by the general term "noise". Interference hampers transinformation from sender to recipient. Interference of noise may be regarded as being irrelevant information which the recipient must separate from relevant information. Procedures designed to protect the transmission against noise-induced errors consist in the development of an interference-proof code. A primitive form of code would repeat every sign two or even three times. While this would enable errors in transmission to be recognized and corrected at once, it would also cut down the information flow rate and generate redundancy. Any anti-interference device increases message length and reduces the information flow rate.

1.2.7 Surprise Value

The psychological phenomenon of surprise is observed whenever an event occurs which has a relatively low probability of occurrence with respect to the possible events (signs) of the field. Frank (1964) takes as the measure of surprise value the ratio of the information of event x_j to the mean uncertainty of field X.

$$s(x_j) = \frac{i(x_j)}{H(X)}. \qquad (1\text{--}29)$$

For relatively rare events of a field, the surprise value is greater than 1, and for relatively frequent events, it is smaller than 1.

Thus, for example C in 1.2.3—results of tossing a cigarette pack—the surprise value of the three alternative outcomes in the example is as follows:

largest face $\qquad s(x_1) = \dfrac{0.322}{0.815} = 0.395,$

medium-sized face $\quad s(x_2) = \dfrac{2.474}{0.815} = 3.03,$

small face $\qquad s(x_3) = \dfrac{5.644}{0.815} = 6.92.$

If a definite event is expected with high probability, perception will often occur in the repertory created by the category formation of the two supersigns:

$x_1 =$ "expected event", probability p_1,
$x_2 =$ "unexpected event", probability p_2.

The surprise value of an event from the category of unexpected events is then

$$s(x_2) = \frac{\mathrm{ld}\,\dfrac{1}{p_2}}{p_1\,\mathrm{ld}\,\dfrac{1}{p_1} + p_2\,\mathrm{ld}\,\dfrac{1}{p_2}}. \tag{1–30}$$

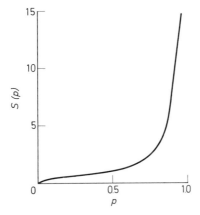

Fig. 1.10   Surprise value of an unexpected event if the expected event has probability p.

2 Measurement of the Information of Written Language and the Concept of Subjective Information

2.1 Introduction

Teaching and education are processes of communication. Educational theory is concerned with the communication process itself as well as with the cognitive changes brought about by this process. By far the greatest part of this communication is conveyed through speech and writing. Here we take the term "written language" to include mathematical, technical and similar symbols, also drawings and diagrams. In this chapter, the measurement of the information in written language is emphasized for two reasons:

a) The transmission of information via printed texts plays a large part in teaching, study and education. Textbooks, handbooks, source-books and reference works are used for this purpose. Today, on an increasing scale, programmed teaching texts are being introduced with the aim of making teaching objective. Besides instruction in reading, the traditional cultural skill—and for our purposes reading is the ability to code phonetic symbols into written symbols and vice versa—there is also instruction in the symbolic languages of mathematics, the natural sciences, technology and other areas of life. The application of information theory to written language opens up a defined and bounded set of pedagogical problems.

b) At present there are still difficulties in attempting a differentiated and direct analysis of the written language by information theory. However, it is feasible to transcribe into written language the verbal communications which occur in the course of educational processes. Compared with direct communication, transcribed speech represents a loss, since it cannot express that part of the information flow between teacher and student which is conveyed by intonation, emphasis, and dynamics, or by gestures and mime. Nevertheless, a large proportion of the information survives transcription. Thus, teaching protocols can be used in the science of education for the analysis of instructional strategies, processes, and situations. If we can apply information theory to the study of written language, we can also gain indirect access to spoken communication via transcription.

Let us add that many of the conclusions which can be drawn from an analysis of information uptake and processing in written language may be applied directly to the spoken language.

The information of written language will first be investigated in 2.2 by means of frequency statistics, which allows a numerical value to be assigned to the stochastic interdependence of sequences of letters within the written language. The statistical analysis of the language will then be extended to words and sequences of words, ignoring at this stage the meaning of the linguistic symbols.

Section 2.3 will deal with the transition from the statistical analysis of language to an *empirical* determination of the information of symbol sequences for human beings as recipients.

In Section 2.4 we introduce the concept of subjective information and hence highlight the empirically observable variables so that we can investigate the interaction between a specific recipient and a given text. When the differences in the information of texts of varied contents for recipients in various situations and states (age, previous knowledge) become the object of our research, we have reached the core of the problem as it applies to education.

Accordingly, in Section 2.5 a procedure is developed for the determination of subjective information which facilitates the performance of measurements and allows more precision; in 2.6 the procedure is extended to any desired symbol sequence, and finally, simplified procedures are proposed for practical use.

The reader who is not specially interested in mathematical questions may omit Sections 2.5.1 and 2.5.2 where the theoretical foundations of the procedure are set out.

2.2 Statistically Based Procedures

2.2.1   Statistics of Letters and Combinations of Letters

A written text is defined as a sequence of signs consisting of letters, punctuation marks and spaces. In a simplification which ignores the differences between upper and lower case letters and neglects punctuation marks, there are 27 signs in the English alphabet (26 letters + space) having a mean information H_0 per sign of 4.70 bits. However, if we take into account the relative frequency of occurrence of the letters, we have, according to Küpfmüller (1954) and Zemanek (1959), an average mean information H_1 of 4.10 bits per sign for German. Shannon (1951) found for English $H_0 = 4.76$ bits per sign and $H_1 = 4.06$ bits per sign.

To allow for bigrammatic dependence we count the bigrams, compute their statistical frequency and obtain $H_2 = 3.80$ bits per sign for German and, according to Shannon, $H_2 = 3.87$ for English. We then find that $H_2 = H$ (bigram) $- H_1$. But the investigation of trigrammatic or in general n-grammatic dependences encounters difficulties of a practical nature. The number of possible n-grams is r^n. If we wish to establish the statistical frequency of bigrams in texts, then, for a repertory of 27 characters, it will be necessary to count the relative frequency of $(27)^2 = 729$ bigrams. In order to investigate trigrammatic dependence, we would have to determine the frequency statistics of $(27)^3 = 19,683$ different possible trigrams. A statistical analysis of the information loss due to n-grammatic dependence cannot go beyond $n = 5$, even when using computers with large storage capacity since, even so, $(27)^5$ combinations, that is about 15 million, would have to be individually recorded.

2.2.2   The Method of Newman and Gerstman

Newman and Gerstman (1952) devised an elegant way of getting round the difficulties of determining the information of n-grams. Their idea is that, with bigrams, knowing one letter reduces the information of the following letter by an amount $T(i, i+1)$ which we already know as the transinformation of one sign onto the next:

$$T(i, i+1) = 2H_1 - H \text{ (bigram)}. \tag{2-1}$$

T may be obtained from the frequency statistics for bigrams.

In similar fashion we may determine the transinformation of a letter onto a sign which will occur $N-1$ positions later. The two signs, the preceding one and the one occurring $N-1$ positions later, are regarded as a bigram. The entire text is resolved into such bigrams and each bigram is considered as a new sign. Now we can determine frequency statistics for these bigrams and compute their mean information. So long as there is a stochastic dependence between the characters separated by n positions, the information of the bigrams will be less than the sum of the mean information of two mutually independent, separate signs. Since the number of bigrams to be considered is always limited, one may in this manner establish an upper limit for the information of texts without undue computation. The analysis was performed with a punched-tape correlator for a text of 10,000 letters taken from the Bible, Isaiah 29–31 (Authorized Version). Newman and Gerstman found that the transinformation of a sign onto that following $N-1$ positions later decreases with increasing N as

$$T(i, i+N-1) = \frac{H_1}{N^2}. \tag{2-2}$$

The values investigated were $N = 1, 2, 3, 4, 5, 6$ and 10. Newman and Gerstman used a "coefficient of constraint" which may be interpreted as a relative transinformation normalized with respect to H_1:

$$D_N = \frac{T(i, i+N-1)}{H_1}. \qquad (2\text{–}3)$$

In our notation, and taking into account the $N-1$ preceding signs, the conditional information of a letter within a text becomes

$$H_N = H_1 - \sum_2^N T(i, i+N-1) \qquad (2\text{–}4)$$

or

$$H_N = H_1\left(1 - \sum_2^N \frac{1}{N^2}\right). \qquad (2\text{–}5)$$

Extrapolating relation (2–5) gives the limiting value

$$H = \lim_{N \to \infty} H_N = H_1\left(1 - \left(\frac{\pi^2}{6} - 1\right)\right) = 1.69 \text{ bit/sign.} \qquad (2\text{–}6)$$

This proves that sequential dependence extends over long sequences of letters.

2.2.3   Word-Frequency Statistics

In theory, it makes no difference whether we treat a written message as a sequence of words or as a sequence of letters. If we take words as the smallest units in the message, they are then supersigns with respect to the letter repertory. Ideally, a message can be built up of letters when these appear at equal time intervals, as in illuminated signs, or when a new word is added at regular time intervals, as is sometimes done in advertising. The process of perception is, however, facilitated when the message is built up of words. Information uptake during reading of printed texts is a process involving controlled change of code, most of the words being perceived as complete words, and only difficult or unknown words being spelled out letter by letter (see note 2/1). In many languages, for instance ancient Chinese, the word is in any case the smallest element in the written language.

Word-frequency statistics also enable us to compute the average information of individual words in printed texts. For about 10,000 of the most frequently used words in the English language, a value of 10.08

bits/word is obtained; Frank (1969) gives a value of 10.9 bits/word for German (see note 2/2).

For an average word length of 7–8 letters per word, this yields a mean information of 1.5 bits per letter. If we take the word frequencies given by Meier (1964) for the German language, we obtain somewhat lower values, particularly for "basic" texts limited to the vocabulary in most frequent use, whereas "advanced" texts, such as scientific articles, give somewhat higher values owing to the occurrence of rare words.

Bürmann, Frank and Lorenz (1963) carried out empirical research into the information of words as a function of word length. They compiled word-frequency statistics from four scientific articles and computed the information of each individual word on the basis of its frequency. Obviously the value of the information in this case is too low, for the calculation relates to the given repertory of the words used, thus a repertory more limited than the general language. Nevertheless, these calculations revealed an interesting relation, namely that the information of a word increases with word length, while the information of a letter decreases as a function of word length. It shows that words hold more information the longer they are, but that the information increases more slowly than the number of letters.

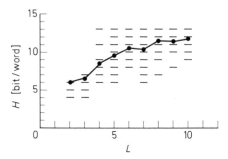

Fig. 2.1   Information of words as a function of word length L in technical sound language (TLD) Bürmann, Frank, Lorenz.

The procedures so far discussed were based upon purely statistical methods, taking into account only the statistical dependences of sequences of letters or the frequency statistics of words. They yield information values that must be considered the upper limit. In fact, textual information will be further restricted both by grammatical constraints and by the context, that is, the situation in which the message is given. Moreover, these procedures do not take into account that the information of a given text for a given addressee depends on his prior knowledge and the level of competence required to understand the text. Viewed in this light, these procedures remain in the domain of validity of mathematical information theory, where the receiver of the message is assumed to have no competence beyond the recognition of statistical relationships, which can just as well be done by a machine.

2.3   Shannon's Guessing-Game Method

In view of the difficulties attending statistical analysis of n-grammatic dependences, Shannon (1951) devised a method for measuring the information reduction in written language due to sequential constraints imposed by linguistic restrictions on word and sentence formation. This was to determine the uncertainty in human subjects concerning the continuation of letter sequences. He supposed the subject to have an internal but unconscious knowledge of sequential dependences which would facilitate prediction of letter sequences.

Shannon's Procedure: A subject attempts to predict the first letter of a random sample of text. The tester says "right" or "wrong". If he was wrong, the test continues until the correct letter has been called. The number of attempts necessary to guess the correct letter are noted for this letter. He then proceeds to the second letter. Here too, the attempts are repeated until the second letter has been correctly guessed. The entire sample of text will be predicted in this way, letter by letter. Shannon carried out such experiments for the first 15 letters and the one hundredth letter of his text samples. It is assumed that the subject carries out an optimum prediction strategy, that is, he always attempts to predict the letter which is most probable by reason of the preceding letter sequence. The method further assumes that the subject will try to minimize the number of predictions. Shannon used random samples of prose from *Finnigan's Wake* for his experiments. As to his subjects, he chose from a large group of persons those who had provided the best prediction results in preliminary tests, that is, those who required the fewest prediction attempts.

It is immediately obvious that the number of prediction attempts V_K for text passage k represents a measure of the uncertainty concerning the character at passage k. Now, Shannon shows that one may determine limiting values for the information of a text if the number of guesses for each letter is known.

The derivation of the upper limit is based on the following considerations:

Let us suppose sender and recipient to be two idealized identical twins, completely similar in their intellectual make-up. Then they might also be able to transmit the information contained in the letter sequence if sender told recipient, in lieu of the letter, how many attempts he would need to guess this letter.

Let a text begin as follows: "The window is cl..."

The next letter is to be predicted. Because the sender's intellectual make-up is exactly the same as the recipient's, he knows the latter expects first of all "o" ("the window is closed") and only as a second thought "e" ("the window is clean"). He can transmit the information contained in the "e" by telling the recipient: "It is not the character you think most probable, but the one you think next most probable." Even though there might be practical difficulties in the realization of such a transmission/reception scheme, theoretically it is quite feasible. Thus, the entire information of the message consisting of the initial letter sequence would be contained in the sequence of numbers representing guesses for each letter. Shannon calls this number sequence the "reduced text". In reduced texts for continuous textual material by far the largest number of guesses were right first time, i.e. about 75 %. Thus, the number 1 makes up most of the reduced text. The numbers 2, 3, 4 and 5 are still relatively frequent; higher numbers do occur, but only rarely. The mean information of this number sequence may now be computed from the frequency distribution of the numbers. Since the sequence contains the entire information of the text, the information of the text cannot be greater, but only equal or less. This gives the upper limit for the information of the text.

If h_k is the relative frequency of signs requiring k attempts for correct prediction, then the upper limit will be

$$H_{max} = \sum_{k=1}^{r} h_k \, \mathrm{ld} \, \frac{1}{h_k}. \qquad (2-7)$$

Somewhat more complex considerations are required for the derivation of the lower limit. (For an elementary proof, see Weltner, 1965.) Fundamentally, one assumes that there is a definite number of equally probable alternatives for each text position. For a total of r symbols there would then be r such categories. One can further show that, on the basis of this distribution of guesses, one may achieve a distribution of the individual signs onto those r categories. The information for that distribution can be determined and the computation gives the expression

$$H_{min} = \sum_{k=1}^{r} k \, (h_k - h_{k-1}) \, \mathrm{ld} \, (k). \qquad (2-8)$$

Shannon provides the values shown in Fig. 2.2 for the upper and lower information limits from his own experiments (1 subject, 100 random text samples, prediction of the first 15 and the 100th sign).

The information of a sign depends on the number of the preceding signs known. It falls initially and then approaches asymptotically a value

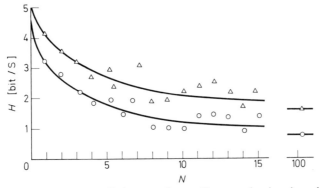

Fig. 2.2 Information of letters, limits according to Shannon showing dependence on knowledge of the number N of preceding symbols.

that might be reached when the subject knows 99 preceding letters. The information then lies between 0.6 and 1.3 bits. The limits for the information per sign are wide apart. Shannon supposes that the true value of information per sign is closer to the upper than the lower value because the subject's situation is better approximated by the model for calculating the upper limit than by the rather artificial one for the lower limit. The proportion of signs correctly guessed at the first attempt is surprisingly high, reaching approximately 80% when 99 preceding characters are known.

Burton and Licklider (1955) went further and investigated the number of preceding signs at which the information of a letter approaches a limit. Using Shannon's guessing-game technique and English prose texts, they carried out experiments in which the subjects knew respectively 1, 2, 4, 8, 16, 32, 64, 128, or 10,000 of the preceding signs.

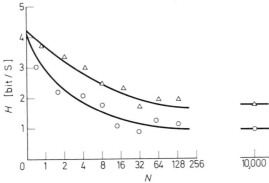

Fig. 2.3 Information of letters, dependence on knowledge of preceding symbols (Burton and Licklider).

The result is shown in Fig. 2.3. The information limit is reached at about 32 preceding signs, according to their experimental data. This implies that prediction of a letter is facilitated only by a knowledge of 5 or 6 preceding words. For English prose texts, it cannot be shown that knowing more than 6 preceding words improves prediction any further.

In another investigation, applying the same guessing-game technique, Carson (1961) determined the information dependence of a letter as a function of its position within the words. These experiments too were carried out on prose texts in English.

Fig. 2.4 shows information as function of letter position. Solid line: words predicted out of context (scrambled texts).

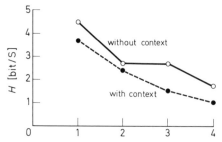

Fig. 2.4   Information of letters as a function of their position within the word, after Carson; values processed.

The first letter has considerably more information than any other. It is striking that the decline in information from the first to the second letter, and from the third to the fourth, is very large, while the third letter contains comparatively more information. Carson explains this statistically confirmed result by the vowel-consonant switch and the fact that a new syllable frequently starts with the third letter. For words within a context, for which therefore a sequence of preceding words is known, values for subjective information are lower—shown by dashed line. Here, though, we see a regular decline in information with word position.

Küpfmüller (1954) carried out the first determination of the information of letters for written German. He skillfully used statements obtained by statistical analysis of syllable and word frequencies, combining them with the results of prediction tests in which the subject predicted words or syllables missing in the text. In this manner one may determine the constraints imposed by the grammatical and semantic context. From the relative proportions of correctly predicted words or syllables Küpfmüller computed the relative redundancy of texts with respect to words and syllables and so was able to supplement the statistical statements.

For German, he obtained a value of 1.6 bits/letter—neglecting the space. He remarked in his paper that the relative redundancy of texts depends on the texts themselves and varies between 0.15 and 0.33. Krah, Kirchberg and Schmädicke (1965) obtained similar results.

Applying Shannon's experimental method, Hansson (1960) and Kolmogorov—the latter quoted in Jaglom (1967)—showed for Swedish and Russian respectively that the average information of the characters of European languages assumes similar values. However, all these experiments are based on prose texts.

Frick and Sumby (1952) investigated radio communication between pilots and control towers and obtained for this standardized language an information of 0.2 bits/sign. The redundancy in this language means greater transmission security.

The initial aim of all these investigations was to obtain statements about the information value of the letters in the language in question. In selecting subjects, Shannon's principle was observed, namely to pre-select them so as to use persons with the fewest wrong predictions in preliminary guessing tests. If the statements are to apply to written language in general, then the differences between the various texts, and those in the prediction abilities of the various subjects, must be regarded as undesirable sources of error in the investigations. Attneave (1959) on the other hand pointed out that information determination by means of guessing procedures is well suited for a study of the differences arising from different levels of language fluency, vocabulary and factual knowledge in the subjects used.

2.4   The Concept of Subjective Information

The information of a given text, whether it be a prose text, a letter, a telegram, or a school book, depends not only on the statistical constraint between the individual characters but much more on the recipient's expectation values, that is, on his knowledge. Let us assume, for instance, that we are presenting the text of a telegram, "Peter arrived yesterday. Doing well." in a guessing test. This text contains more information for the telegraph operator, who at first does not know whether this is a business, technical or personal telegram, than for the recipient, who already knows that the sender's wife is expecting a baby and that the name is to be either Peter or Karin.

Therefore the information of a sequence of signs depends quite decisively upon the state of mind of the receiver, on his command of the language, on his knowledge of the circumstances, and on his situation when he receives the message. Purely statistical methods which describe the relationships between letter sequences do not allow for an intelligent

recipient with a knowledge of the world, and are unable to take cogniz-
ance of the semantic level.

The practical difficulties in statistically determining the information
of n-grams where n is equal to or greater than 4, led Shannon to determine empirically the information in letter sequences. Shannon is concerned with the stochastic relationship between letter sequences that are
valid for language in general. Therefore he establishes

1. an ideal language as a unifying set for all texts, taking a prose text
as an approximation;

2. an ideal reader who meets the following requirements: possesses
a wide knowledge of the statistical rules of the language and of the grammatical constraints upon word-sequence probabilities. These requirements
are violated once the reader has any knowledge whatsoever about the
content of the text.

This concept is useless for the treatment of educational problems.
Here the problem is the exact opposite, namely, the information of texts
of different degrees of difficulty addressed to certain groups differing in
age, command of language and previous knowledge. Thus the information
of a given text is considered as a measure of the relationship between text
and recipient, as opposed to a measure based on statistical foundations,
and is therefore called subjective information (von Cube, 1965; Frank,
1964; Weltner, 1964). The concept of subjective information may also
be applied to the analysis of processes of cognitive structuring (see Bongard, 1966; Kharkevich, 1964; Klix, 1968 and Steinbuch, 1960).

The transition to the concept of subjective information gives access
to a whole range of problems relevant to education. If the subjective information of a textbook is known, it is possible to quantify the subjective
degree of difficulty of the teaching material or of its presentation. The
subjective information of the transcribed utterances of a teacher talking
to his pupils allows the problem of the teaching language appropriate
to the pupils' age to be expressed quantitatively. On the basis of the subjective information of instructional material as a function of teaching,
it is possible to develop ways of measuring learning success, the results
of which may be expressed as a measure of information and analyzed
according to information theory. The measurement of subjective information enables cognitive processes, such as occur when messages are
received, to be recognized. One may analyze the functional mechanism
of language barriers by investigating the subjective information of random samples of text in the domains of ordinary speech (public language,
restricted code) and in formal language (elaborated code).

Thus the concept of subjective information provides a transition by
means of which the semantic aspect of communication via language,

and basically the pragmatic aspect, too, may be taken into account. This brings us to the area of problems relevant to education.

There is thus a shift in the problem: from studying the statistical dependence of language we now have to determine subjective expectation values for the probability of events or sequences of events. Conversely, therefore, subjective information is a measure of the recipient's uncertainty regarding a field of events.

In order to carry out this program, we develop in the following sections procedures for measuring subjective information which are flexible enough to be adapted to changing statements of the problem and which allow it to be formulated more precisely than was possible by the procedures hitherto used. Moreover, these procedures, because they are simplified, cut down the time and effort required for research.

2.5   Digitizing Prediction by Means of Branching Diagrams

Branching diagrams are often used in coding and information theory for the graphical solution of problems of classification and coding. Dichotomy-based branching trees are used in particular for binary coding and its optimization (Huffmann, 1952).

Basically, we wish to use such branching diagrams as heuristic aids in order to determine empirically the subjective information of alternative decisions (Weltner, 1964). In this way branching diagrams may be used for prediction experiments. The prediction of a text with the aid of a branching diagram proceeds in the following fashion:

The subject knows the preceding text consisting of n letters. The branching diagram in Fig. 2.5 is available to him for the purpose of prediction.

The path to every letter has five branching or decision points. The vowels, followed by the consonants, are arranged in alphabetical order reading from left to right. On the far right are word spacer, period, comma, semicolon, hyphen, and question mark, all of which are to be considered as symbols in their own right. In the symbol repertory so defined, each

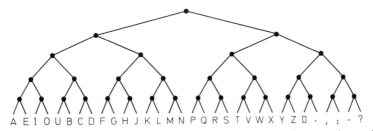

Fig. 2.5   Branching diagram for letter prediction with word spacer and punctuation marks.

symbol has a maximum information of 5 bits. The subject states at the first decision point whether he expects the continuation to be in the right or left half of the diagram. The tester then has two possible answers: "correct" or "other side". This defines the next decision point, which is handled in the same manner except that the repertory is now restricted. Every symbol is thus predicted with five guesses and the number of errors for each letter is recorded. Each guess halves the repertory of the remaining letters which could be predicted. A detailed account of this procedure will be found in section 5.2.

The first obvious advantage of this kind of prediction experiment is that it is faster. Whereas the prediction of a letter by Shannon's guessing-game method takes on average 20 seconds, the time in this instance is cut to about 10 seconds. The advantage is two-fold, since on the one hand longer samples of text can be analyzed and on the other hand unproductive guessing is reduced for information-rich passages of the text. At such passages the subject readily suffers fatigue and frustration when no longer able to think of reasonable alternatives. Furthermore, when the guessing process is speeded up, the subject retains a better idea of the context and grammatical coherence.

To make sure that during prediction experiments subjects will indeed keep to the requirement that grammatically reasonable continuations be chosen, it is important in experiments using branching diagrams to make the subject state the continuation of the word or words on which the prediction is based.

When a complex word or a sequence of letters is correctly predicted in this type of test, this prediction may be noted and counted as the correct one for a series of alternative decisions.

Example. If the known sequence of letters is "Infor . . . ." and the subject predicts at the first division in the branching tree: "Right. I expect: information", and if this is the correct prediction of the entire word, the tester can note the word. Working in this way, the subject makes a large number of accurate predictions "en bloc".

In this experimental technique the branching diagram is used for prediction only when there is real uncertainty about the continuation. This means that testing can be done without wearying the subject with unnecessary difficulties which do not serve any real purpose.

Once tests have revealed the number of hints required for predicting the entire text, then upper and lower limits may be obtained for the information of the text.

The subjective information of letter sequences is not the final goal but rather an intermediate step in determining the information of word sequences and their complex coded messages. Just as the subjective information of letters is more easily obtained by digitizing prediction by means of a branching diagram, so the prediction of letters facilitates the approach to the subjective information of words.

As the following considerations show, the mean information per sign is not altered by digitizing prediction and obtaining the information at the decision points:

Let there be r elements with probabilities p_j, then the mean information is

$$H = \sum_{j=1}^{r} P_j \, \mathrm{ld} \, \frac{1}{P_j} \qquad (2\text{–}8)$$

Two elements z_1 and z_2 with probabilities p_1 and p_2 contribute to the mean information the amount

$$h = p_1 \, \mathrm{ld} \, \frac{1}{p_1} + p_2 \, \mathrm{ld} \, \frac{1}{p_2}. \qquad (2\text{–}9)$$

Let the information be split into two parts, which can be determined successively:

1. The information h_1 of the decision point with probability $p_{12} = p_1 + p_2$,

$$h_1 = (p_1 + p_2) \cdot \mathrm{ld} \, \frac{1}{(p_1 + p_2)}. \qquad (2\text{–}10)$$

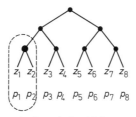

$$\begin{array}{cccccccc} z_1 & z_2 & z_3 & z_4 & z_5 & z_6 & z_7 & z_8 \\ p_1 & p_2 & p_3 & p_4 & p_5 & p_6 & p_7 & p_8 \end{array}$$

Fig. 2.6 Branching diagram for 8 symbols which are combinations of two symbols.

2. The conditional information h_2 of both elements, assuming the repertory is diminished because of the knowledge of the decision point,

$$h_2 = (p_1 + p_2)\left[\frac{p_1}{p_1 + p_2} \cdot \mathrm{ld}\left(\frac{p_1 + p_2}{p_1}\right) + \frac{p_2}{p_1 + p_2} \cdot \mathrm{ld}\left(\frac{p_1 + p_2}{p_2}\right) \right], \qquad (2\text{–}11)$$

$$h_2 = \left[p_1 \cdot \mathrm{ld} \, \frac{1}{p_1} + p_2 \, \mathrm{ld} \, \frac{1}{p_2} \right] - \left[(p_1 + p_2) \, \mathrm{ld} \, \frac{1}{(p_1 + p_2)} \right]. \qquad (2\text{–}12)$$

The conditional information h_2 is equal to the information of the two elements minus h_1. The sum of the two information components is

$$h = h_1 + h_2 = p_1 \, \mathrm{ld} \, \frac{1}{p_1} + p_2 \, \mathrm{ld} \, \frac{1}{p_2}. \qquad (2\text{–}13)$$

The sum is equal to the initial information of both elements. The entire branching diagram may be built up from the elements in similar fashion. We have shown that for one combination the total information does not change. We compute the information of the digitized decisions at the decision points and thus successively limit the repertory. This gives us the mean information of the r elements. When prediction has been repeated n times, the individual decision points will be rated in accordance with their probability.

2.5.1   Derivation of Limits for Subjective Information by Means of Digitized Prediction

When Shannon's procedure is used for the empirical determination of subjective information, practical difficulties are encountered in the case of subjectively information-rich letter sequences because, where there is great uncertainty, many prediction attempts are required before the correct letter is predicted. Enlarging the repertory, which is quite feasible in principle, will only increase these difficulties and will, in fact, block the process. These difficulties can be bypassed by digitizing prediction by means of branching diagrams, and this method has the further advantage that one and the same approach enables the subjective information to be confined within narrower bounds.

When branching diagrams are used, the prediction of a text of Z letters plus additional symbols is achieved through prediction at a total of N decision points. In the example under consideration, $N = 5 \cdot Z$. As an empirical result, we obtain the number N_F of false predictions. What statement can then be made concerning the subjective information of these N predictions? The following considerations are based on the assumption that subjects will seek to minimize the number of false decisions at every step and will therefore muster their knowledge of the grammatical, syntactic and contextual relationships in order to predict at every branching the subjectively most probable of the alternative continuations.

Let us consider a decision at a branching point:

We are seeking the subjective probabilities p_1 and p_2 for the two alternatives. These are unknown. According to the guessing strategy, the subject chooses the subjectively more probable continuation. Let that one be p_1. The probability of being wrong is p_2 and lies between 0 and 0.5. The probability of *error* will be called p_e since the considerations involved rest upon the determination of p_e. If there were N decisions with the same p_e, we could determine p_e from the empirically obtained number of observed wrong decisions as the limiting value of their relative frequency.

$$p_e = \lim_{N \to \infty} \frac{N_F}{N} . \tag{2-14}$$

Fig. 2.7

Thus one might obtain the subjective information from

$$H(p_1) = p_1 \, \mathrm{ld} \, \frac{1}{p_e} + (1 - p_1) \, \mathrm{ld} \, \frac{1}{1 - p_e}. \qquad (2\text{-}15)$$

In reality, however, we are dealing, not with a constant probability of error during N decisions, but with context-dependent and therefore varying subjective probabilities of error at the N decision points.

In the following considerations (Weltner, 1967c) we begin by assuming that we derive from some source the knowledge of the probability of error for each decision, although in fact we do not have it. Were we to possess such knowledge, then we might rearrange all decisions and place them in order, not of their occurrence during the experiments, but according to increasing subjective probability of error. This would give us a regular progression of steps of increasing p_e.

The steps can rise from 0 to 0.5. Because of the assumptions made about the guessing strategy, values in excess of 0.5 are impossible. The number of steps is at most N—when all probabilities of error are different —or equal to T, when decisions with the same p_e can be placed together in one or more steps. As an approximation, such summations may be carried out for given intervals of p_e.

The consideration relating to the determination of p_e can now be applied to a single step.

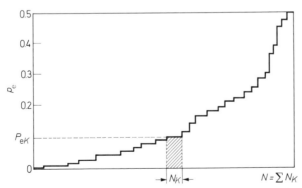

Fig. 2.8   Subjective probabilities error of p_{ek} rearranged in order of increasing p_e (stepped curve).

Let N_k be the number of decisions at step k, and N_{Fk} the number of false decisions; then for large N and hence sufficiently large N_k:

$$p_{ek} = \frac{N_{Fk}}{N_k}. \qquad (2\text{–}16)$$

The area below step k is then

$$N_{Fk} = p_{ek} \cdot N_k. \qquad (2\text{–}17)$$

The entire area below the stepped curve is given by

$$N_F = \sum_{K=1}^{T} p_{ek} N_k. \qquad (2\text{–}18)$$

The real course of the curve remains unknown, yet the area below the curve can be empirically determined as the number of wrong decisions N_F. Of course, we have assumed that N is very large, and we then determine the underlying expectation probabilities from the empirically determinable relative frequencies. The error deriving from N being finite is considered as a random error and is neglected here (note 2/3).

The problem may now be reduced to this question:

Given the boundary condition of constant area, can we assign upper and lower limits to the information of the N decisions represented by the stepped curve?

One can show that:

1. The information assumes its minimum when the only values for p_e are 0 and 0.5.

2. The information assumes its maximum when all p_e are equal.

The information of the (unknown) distribution of the probabilities of error according to the stepped curve is

$$I = \sum_{K=1}^{N} h(p_{ek}). \qquad (2\text{–}19)$$

In the following arguments we shall always be dealing with subjective probabilities of error. To simplify the notation, the subscript e denoting *error* probabilities will be omitted. Then we have

$$h(p) = p \cdot \mathrm{ld}\,\frac{1}{p} + (1-p) \cdot \mathrm{ld}\,\frac{1}{(1-p)}. \qquad (2\text{–}20)$$

The curve of the information h as a function of the error probability p is given in Fig. 2.9.

The derivative

$$\frac{dh}{dp} = \mathrm{ld}\,\frac{1-p}{p} \qquad (2\text{–}21)$$

of this function is positive and monotonic decreasing (see Fig. 2.10) in the entire domain

$$0 < p \le 0.5. \qquad (2\text{–}22)$$

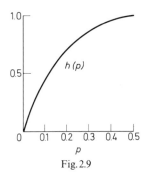

Fig. 2.9

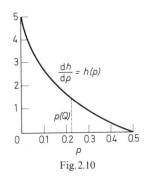

Fig. 2.10

Lower Limit. We now consider a variation in the distribution of the p_k's represented by the stepped curve, observing the boundary condition of constant area below the curve. The variation shall be such that it intersects the stepped curve at point Q, and lies below the original curve on the left and above it on the right (see Fig. 2.11)

For the variation of the p_k's,

$$\sum_{K=1}^{N} \delta p_k = 0. \tag{2–23}$$

To the left of Q, the δp_k are negative, and to the right they are positive.

The following conditions then apply to the two domains separated by Q:

If $\qquad 0 < k < Q, \qquad$ then $\delta p_k \leq 0; \dfrac{dh}{dp} \geq \dfrac{dh}{dp}(p_Q);$ $\qquad$ (2–24)

if

$$Q < k < N, \qquad \text{then } \delta p_k \geq 0; \frac{dh}{dp} \leq \frac{dh}{dp}(p_Q). \tag{2–25}$$

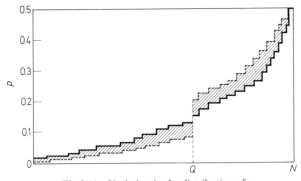

Fig. 2.11   Variation in the distribution of p_k.

One then obtains for the information of the varied distribution p_k

$$I = \sum_{k=1}^{N} h\,(p_k + \delta p_k) = I_0 + \sum_{K=1}^{N} \frac{dh}{dp}\,(p_k)\,\delta p_k. \tag{2–26}$$

The sum may be divided into two parts. Then the change in information becomes

$$\delta I = I - I_0 = \sum_{K=1}^{Q-1} \frac{dh}{dp}\,(p_k)\,\delta p_k + \sum_{K=Q}^{N} \frac{dh}{dp}\,(p_k)\,\delta p_k \tag{2–27}$$

which is negative on account of (2–24) and (2–25). The sums of the δp_k's to the left and to the right of Q are the same but of opposite signs, whereas in the sums of (2–27) the factor for the left side is larger than for the right side. The given variation therefore yields

$$\delta I \leq 0. \tag{2–28}$$

Through a series of such variations one may always obtain a distribution such that the p_k vanish up to point Q and thereafter assume the value 0.5. The fact that the area under the curve is constant together with (2–18) gives the condition for Q:

$$Q = N - 2N_F. \tag{2–29}$$

For every variation, δI is negative. Therefore we obtain a minimum for the information of this limiting distribution, namely

$$I_{min} = \sum_{k=1}^{N} h\,(p_k) = \sum_{K=Q}^{N} h_k\,(0.5) = 2N_F. \tag{2–30}$$

The average information of decisions is therefore

$$H_{min} = \frac{I_{min}}{N} = \frac{2N_F}{N}. \tag{2–31}$$

Upper Limit. The same approach will lead us to the upper limit; however, we must now reverse the variations in the p_k distribution in the stepped curve shown in 2.11, so that the variation now runs above the original curve to the left of Q and below it to the right. Since this changes only the signs of δp_k, the same proof will show that for any such variation δI will be positive. We reach the limiting case of maximum information when all p_k are equal. This situation corresponds to the well-known theorem which states that the information of an event field assumes a maximum when all events are of equal probability. In this case

$$I_{max} = N \cdot h\left(\frac{N_F}{N}\right). \tag{2–32}$$

Therefore the average information of decisions is given by

$$H_{max} = h\left(\frac{N_F}{N}\right) = \frac{N_F}{N} \operatorname{ld} \frac{N}{N_F} + \left(\frac{N - N_F}{N}\right) \operatorname{ld} \frac{N}{N - N_F}. \quad (2\text{-}33)$$

If, then, we know for a set of N predictions made by means of a branching diagram the number of false decisions N_F, it will be possible to obtain upper and lower limits for the information; see Fig. 2.12.

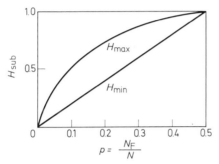

Fig. 2.12 Limits of subjective information H_{sub} per decision point as a function of N_F/N.

The limits are relatively far apart. Now we must ask whether they may be brought closer together. This will be done in the following argument since the general proof already includes the basis for such a refinement. This was also the reason why the proof was set out in that particular manner. The two limiting cases above could have been derived from simpler considerations (Weltner, 1967c).

The branching diagram contains 5 decision points per character. The average information per character is then given by

$$H_{character} = 5 \cdot H_{decision\ pt}. \quad (2\text{-}34)$$

Though the branching diagram in the form so far discussed was developed for the prediction of letter sequences, it is immediately evident that it may be applied to prediction experiments using any kind of branching scheme. If a diagram contains Z decision points the average information per symbol is given by

$$H_{symbol} = Z H_{decision\ pt}. \quad (2\text{-}35)$$

This allows the method to be extended to the determination of the subjective information of any desired repertory.

Shannon had to make two assumptions for deriving the upper and lower limits in his guessing-game procedures:

1st assumption: The subject's prediction strategy aims at minimizing the number of mistakes.

2nd assumption: The thought model of the identical twins whose mental states are exactly the same.

For our derivation, however, only the first assumption is required.

2.5.2   Procedure for a More Exact Determination of Subjective Information

The Method. The derivation of the limits of subjective information was based on an arrangement of N predictions at N decision points according to increasing subjective probability of error. The empirical results allow us to estimate the area under the stepped curve.

We need two things for a more exact determination. First, additional knowledge relating to the shape of the curve, then a method which will make it easier to determine the subjective information from this apparently incomplete knowledge. In order to obtain guide points concerning the shape of the curve, we can modify the guessing tests so that each decision successively indicates:

1. the decision – "left" or "right";
2. a subjective estimate of the probability of error.

In this way we can classify the decisions according to the subjective probabilities of error.

In our empirical experiments, the subject had to indicate his estimate of the likelihood of error by means of a 10-interval scale; Weltner (1968, 1969). The intervals extend from absolute certainty (probability of error $p=0$) via 8 intermediate steps to complete uncertainty (probability of error $p=0.5$). Each prediction can then be noted on a data sheet in the appropriate interval and be classified according to correct or false prediction. The subject gives his subjective likelihood of error as a percentage.

Requiring the subject to state the subjective probability of error should give him some understanding of the order of precedence within the intervals. On the basis of correct and incorrect predictions, N_{correct} and N_F, the genuine subjective probability of error p may be obtained for each interval. When the score sheets were evaluated, two corrections had to be introduced in order to compensate for random errors and mistakes in carrying out the tests.

a) It was noted during counting that sometimes the scorer recorded up to 3% fewer decisions than were called for by the sample of text, though the average of missing entries was under 1%. The missing entries were made up in such a way as to maintain the proportion of entries falling into the intervals and the ratio of correct to incorrect predictions within one interval.

Specimen score sheet

Interval	$K=1$	2	3	4	5	6	7	8	9	10
$p_k\,(\%)$	0	0.1	0.5	1	2	5	10	20	30	50
$N_{correct}$	48	197	41		11	80		32	17	26
N_F		2	2		4	6		8	8	18
N_K	48	199	43		15	86		40	25	44
P_K	0	0.010	0.046		0.266	0.070		0.200	0.320	0.409

$N = N_1 + N_2 + \cdots + N_{10} = 500$ no. of letters $= 100$

b) The empirically obtained probabilities of error must show a monotonic increase. Deviations occurred in intervals holding few entries (interval 5). Such deviations were considered random and were smoothed out by combining a deviant interval having too high an empirical probability of error with the next interval.

The division into 10 intervals proved excessive. In most score sheets, the entries were clustered in 5 to 7 intervals. Despite instructions to use the whole scale, several intervals were frequently left empty. The performance of the test depends upon the subject being capable of classifying the subjective probabilities of error. The fact that only 5 to 7 categories were used agrees with the findings of Pollack and Ficks (1954) relating to the classification of acoustic pitch, and to the findings of Eriksen and Hake (1954) concerning the recognition of the size of squares, and similar experiments which showed that, independently of dimension, an average, subjectively activated classification falls naturally into 6 to 8 categories.

The number of intervals used for the final evaluation was further restricted to 5. The constriction was to provide intervals equally spaced with respect to their mean information. If the information of a decision point extending from 0 to 1 is divided into five equal parts, then we have established 5 domains of this decision point for probabilities of error.

The results were entered in this interval classification in proportion to the empirically determined error probability of the intervals on the

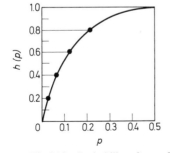

Interval limits	
$h(p)$	p
1,0	0,500
0,8	0,240
0,6	0,145
0,4	0,079
0,2	0,031
0	0

Fig. 2.13   Probability of error for interval limits given in table

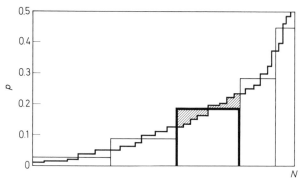

Fig. 2.14   Curve with intervals; decisions rearranged according to increasing p_k.

score sheet, and an average error probability was computed for each of the five intervals on the basis of these entries (note 2/4).

Thus the predictions are first separated according to their error probability and obtained as a monotonic rising classification. In order to show how one may establish narrower limits for the information of the predictions falling within a given interval, we shall consider the third interval in Fig. 2.14.

The true course of a sequence of predictions arranged in order of increasing probability of error is unknown. But we do know the average value of this stepped curve.

Lower Limit. We again take the consideration set up for the derivation of the lower limit of the entire stepped curve. Every distribution of error probability within the third interval, the one we are considering, which runs below the true curve on the left and above it on the right and which intersects the true curve at Q, reduces the information of the predictions. It is assumed that the area below the curve is constant.

We are seeking a curve which reliably fulfills this assumption yet avoids a probability distribution concentrated at the extremes of 0 and 0.5. The unknown true curve may be replaced by one consisting of two steps. For this, the step on the left must have a value greater than 0 but smaller than the lowest point of the curve at the boundary with the second interval which is adjacent to it on the left. The step on the right must have a value smaller than 0.5 but greater than the highest point of the curve at the boundary with the fourth interval which is adjacent to it on the right. Any such substitute curve meets the condition for deriving the lower limit. We may now obtain suitable steps for our empirical intervals from a consideration which takes into account the results present in the neighboring intervals. The average value of the second interval, which adjoins the third interval on the *left*, must surely lie on the interval boundary

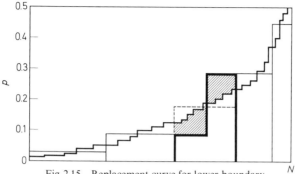

Fig. 2.15   Replacement curve for lower boundary

below the stepped curve. It may coincide with the curve, but only when all p's in the second interval are equal, and even in that case all the conditions for derivation are met; see Fig. 2.15.

The average value of the adjacent interval on the *right* must surely lie on the interval boundary above the highest value of the stepped curve in interval 3. Both values are known empirically. This allows a new lower limit to be given for the subjective information of the decisions entered in the third interval. If these results are summed over the intervals, a new lower limit is obtained for the information of the ensemble of all predictions. This new lower limit lies considerably higher than that obtained from the original consideration.

Calculation. The N_K predictions of the k'th interval must be divided into two parts: $N_{1,k}$ predictions with error probability p_{k-1} and with the information

$$h\,(p_{k-1})=p_{k-1}\ \text{ld}\ \frac{1}{p_{k-1}}+(1-p_{k-1})\ \text{ld}\ \frac{1}{(1-p_{k-1})},$$

and $N_{2,k}$ predictions with error probability p_{k+1} and the information $h\,(p_{k+1})$.

The following condition applies:

$$N_{1,k}+N_{2,k}=N_k.$$

Due to the constancy of the area below all the comparable curves, we obtain:

and

$$N_{1,k}\,(p_k-p_{k-1})=N_{2,k}\,(p_{k+1}-p_k) \qquad (2\text{–}36)$$

$$\Delta p_k = p_{k+1}-p_{k-1} \qquad (2\text{–}37)$$

therefore

$$N_{1,k}=N_k\cdot\frac{(p_{k+1}-p_k)}{\Delta p_k} \qquad (2\text{–}38)$$

$$N_{2,k}=N_k\cdot\frac{(p_k-p_{k-1})}{\Delta p_k}. \qquad (2\text{–}39)$$

This yields the lower limit of information for interval k:

$$I_{k\,min} = N_{1k} \cdot h_{k-1} + N_{2k} \cdot h_{k+1},$$

or

$$I_{k\,min} = N_k \frac{p_{k+1} - p_k}{\Delta p_k} \cdot h_{k-1} + \frac{p_k - p_{k-1}}{\Delta p_k} \cdot h_{k+1} \qquad (2\text{–}40)$$

and therefore for all intervals

$$I_{k\,min} = \sum_{k=1}^{5} e_{k\,min} \qquad (2\text{–}41)$$

Consequently we obtain for the lower limit of the mean information per decision point

$$H_{min} = \frac{I_{min}}{N}. \qquad (2\text{–}42)$$

Upper Limit. The reasoning used to obtain the upper limit of the subjective information of the entire stepped curve also applies to this interval. The information is greatest when all predictions within the interval have an equal probability of error. If we replace the curve within the interval by its average value, then the information of the decisions calculated for this is greater than when the true curve is taken into account:

$$I_{k\,max} = N_k \cdot h_k. \qquad (2\text{–}43)$$

If the upper limit of information is summed over the various intervals, we obtain an upper limit for the whole information:

$$I_{max} = \sum_{k=1}^{5} N_k \cdot h_k. \qquad (2\text{–}44)$$

Then the upper limit for the mean information per decision point is

$$H_{max} = \frac{I_{max}}{N}. \qquad (2\text{–}45)$$

The new upper limit is lower than the original one because the errors incurred in forming the average values within the intervals are smaller than when we take an average value for the entire curve. Kolmogorov (note 2/5) reported a lowering of the upper limit for Shannon's guessing-game method and he took this lower value to be the true one.

Experimental Results. The empirical experiments were based on one prose text (G. Weisenborn's short story, "*Zwei Männer*") and on one passage from a programmed textbook (*Heat I: Temperature*). Two random samples were taken from each text.

Weisenborn: sample A: 85 symbols, 19 subjects,
                      sample B: 82 symbols, 19 subjects,
programmed text: sample A: 68 symbols, 20 subjects,
                      sample B: 68 symbols, 20 subjects,

The experiments were carried out on two days. Test duration per subject and per sample was about 40 minutes.

There are four values for each subject and for each text sample: the original upper and lower limits of the subjective information and the narrower limits calculated according to the new procedure. For sample calculation, see note (2/6).

The results are given in Fig. 2.16: the new limits are joined by a line and it is clear that the upper limit is considerably lowered while the lower limit is considerably raised. At the same time they show a good deal of variance; it is therefore necessary to check whether this may be interpreted as random variance. A total of four text samples were investigated here; the variance also occurs for each text sample within the group of subjects.

The calculation is based on the empirical probability of error in 5 intervals. The determination of the empirical probability of error is subject to random error. The standard deviation is:

$$\delta p_k = \sqrt{N_k \cdot p_k \cdot (1 - p_k)}. \qquad (2\text{--}46)$$

As the entries N_k in the score sheets also showed variance between intervals, we established an average score sheet comprising the mean value of the entries in all sheets.

A somewhat tedious method allows computation by the law of cumulative error of the upper limit

$$H_{max} = \frac{1}{N} \sum_{K=1}^{5} N_k \cdot h(p_k) \qquad (2\text{--}47)$$

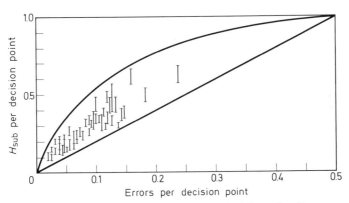

Fig. 2.16   Narrower boundaries of subjective information H_{sub}.

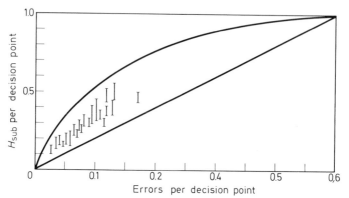

Fig. 2.17   Narrower boundaries for H_{sub}. Combination of two score sheets.

and of the lower limit

$$H_{\text{min}} = \frac{1}{N_K} \sum_{K=1}^{5} N_k \left[\frac{p_{k+1} - p_k}{\Delta p_k} \cdot h(p_{k-1}) + \frac{p_k - p_{k-1}}{\Delta p_k} \cdot h(p_{k+1}) \right] \quad (2\text{–}48)$$

of errors in single determinations.

This gives values of 0.17 bit per character for the upper limit and 0.18 bit per character for the lower limit. Thus the variance to be expected from the law of cumulative error lies within the order of magnitude of the observed variance.

In order to minimize this random error, we combined the results from two score sheets. The scores for each text sample were arranged in order of increasing total number of incorrect decisions; the entries from two successive sheets were then summed and new limits determined for them; see Fig. 2.17.

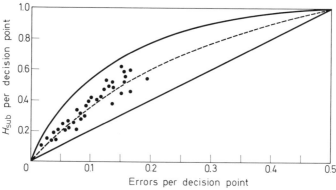

Fig. 2.18   Average values of H_{sub} for narrower limits; average-value curve of original limits of H_{sub}.

The random errors cancel out. If we compare the average value of the lowered upper limits and raised lower limits with the average values of the original limits, the two values are found to be surprisingly close; see Fig. 2.18.

The measured values lie so close to the average-value curve that we may for the time being take this curve as the best estimate of subjective information. The average deviation of the single measurement δ_H from the average-value curve is 0.13 bit. This result is convenient because there is an analytic expression for the average-value curve which gives the information as a function of the average number of errors per decision point.

$$H_{sub} \text{(decision point)} = \frac{1}{2}\left[p \operatorname{ld} \frac{1}{p} + (1-p) \operatorname{ld} \frac{1}{(1-p)} + 2p \right] \quad (2\text{--}49)$$

where $p = N_F/N$.

The influence of interval distribution upon the convergence of the procedure was determined in a separate check calculation. The size of the interval distribution and the definition of interval boundaries are both arbitrary to begin with. The check shows that the procedure converges rapidly and that even division into four intervals leads to satisfactory convergence, irrespective of the principles governing the division; see note (2/7).

Summary. The result of investigating the exact value of subjective information is that for practical purposes it coincides with the average value of the original upper and lower limits. If we take this result as our base, we can already make a more precise statement concerning the true value of subjective information on the basis of the determination of subjective information from the original branching diagram (which gives only the relative proportion of false predictions). The average value may be taken as the empirical calibration curve for which there is an analytical expression, although it is not theoretically supported. Thus, we may define the subjective information H_{sub} directly as a function of the empirically determined relation between correct and false predictions. Unless we explicitly state the contrary, H_{sub} will always be meant when we are discussing below the results of empirical tests. This applies also to the values quoted in older publications as H_{min}. A table and an accurate curve $H_{sub} = f(p)$ will be found in 5.5.

2.5.3 Subjective Information of Different Texts; Age Dependence; Intelligence Dependence

2.5.3.1 H_{sub} as a Function of the Text

For subjects from the same population the subjective information is a function of the text. It is not a value which is characteristic for the written language; on the contrary, it has a considerable range of variation. Fig.

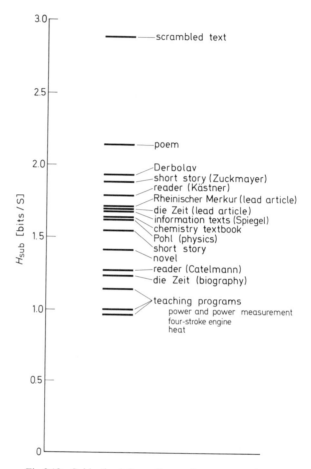

Fig. 2.19   Subjective information, various texts, students.

2.19 sets out the results for a variety of texts: prose, newspapers, ordinary textbooks, programmed textbooks. The subjects were Teacher Training College students.

The differences in H_{sub} are not of a random nature; the standard deviation of a single measurement averages 0.1 bit/character; see table and note (2/8). Passages from ordinary textbooks contain twice as much subjective information as those from programmed textbooks. Narrative prose texts lie within the range 1.2–1.7 bits/symbol. These results are compatible with those obtained by Küpfmüller for German and by Shannon, Carson, also Newman and Gerstman for English. It is interesting that newspaper reports have a relatively high subjective information. This is also true of sophisticated literary texts (Weltner, 1967 a). The least information is contained in programmed teaching texts, the most in what we call "scrambled" texts. Scrambled texts are sequences of words without coherent content or grammar. They are obtained by randomly selecting words from a longer text and then arranging them in random order. Scrambled texts are found to contain nearly twice as much subjective information as texts which possess grammatical and contextual coherence. These word sequences represent a Markov chain without stochastic dependence.

In the absence of measurement errors, when subjective information values obtained for meaningful texts approach those of scrambled texts, we must conclude that the subjects either have not grasped the grammatical relationships, or do not understand the subject matter of the meanings and statements coded by the text. In the absence of such clues enabling the information of a sequence of words to be reduced, it can happen that word sequences which objectively do obey the rules of grammar and in fact are codings which make good sense, might as well be scrambled texts as far as the percipient is concerned. This may be approximately the case with textbook texts when these are of too high a level of difficulty for the reader, because the repertory of words and meanings used is for the most part unknown to the recipient.

2.5.3.2 H_{sub} as a Function of Age

The age dependence of the subjective information of prose texts was studied in school classes, the reading texts being those appropriate to the fifth and eighth school years. The subjects in each test group comprised eight pupils from classes 5–10 of a junior high school (Realschule). H_{sub}

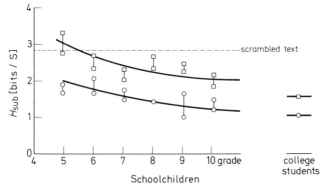

Fig. 2.20   Age dependence of the subjective information of prose texts.   □ Kästner; ○ Catelmann.

decreases with increasing school age and moves asymptotically towards a boundary value, both for a sophisticated description of landscape (Erhard Kästner: "*Die Wüste*") and for a narrative text (Catelmann: "*Der Tierquäler*"); see Fig. 2.20; note (2/9).

The measured values on the right show H_{sub} of the same texts for Teacher Training College students and hence the approximate asymptote. H_{sub} for scrambled texts is entered at the top of the graph. H_{sub} for children in their 5th school year lies above this value, so indicating that this text is using a word repertory and a repertory of grammatical relations which we ought not to expect the reader to be familiar with. This is a case where the sender and the recipient do not have access to even approximately the same repertory of signs.

2.5.3.3 H_{sub} as a Function of the Recipient's Intelligence

If the subjective information of texts is to be measured on the one hand as a function of the text and on the other as a function of the recipient's state of mind, then obviously we must also investigate the influence of intelligence upon subjective information.

This is a question of fundamental significance. For the recipient, each text represents the realization of one message out of a virtually infinite number of messages with varying probability profiles. The intelligence structure of a recipient, on the other hand, is a fairly constant value which can distinguish him significantly from other recipients. The investigation of this problem is also of interest relative to the variance which occurs in our measurements. This variance can have at least two mutually independent causes:

1. the variance of the usually short random samples of text relative to the average value of the text;

2. the variance of the subjective information consequent upon the different intelligence structures of the subjects.

Two series of tests were carried out with 40 subjects, the subjective information of each of four random samples of text being measured for a group of 20 students. The more exact guessing procedure was used for two text samples and a simplified method for the other two. The simplified procedure will be described in the next section. The results of the rank correlation (Speareman correlation) between the various IST subtests according to Amthauer and the subjective information are low-valued and without significance for the entire text. To some extent the low correlations are due to the homogeneity of the test population, which had a mean IQ of 112 with a standard deviation of 5.05. For the population in-

Correlation: IST (Amthauer)—subjective information H_{sub}.
Guessing-game procedure: simplified method (letters), branching diagram.
Text: M. Anger, "*Die heimliche Verlobung*", short story. K. Weltner,
"*Wärmelehre*", teaching program, experimental version.

		Rank correlation coefficient			
		text sample	short story	text sample	teaching program
		a	b	c	d
	no. of symbols	$s=129$	$s=142$	$s=93$	$s=68$
	no. of subjects	20	20	20	20
IST (Amthauer)	SE	0.10	0.48	-0.13	0.25
	WA	0.36	0.18	0.0	-0.28
	AN	0.26	0.18	-0.11	0.02
	GE	0.18	-0.42	-0.02	0.08
	ME	0.02	0.06	0.21	0.35
	RA	0.35	0.42	0.34	-0.05
	ZR	0.16	0.05	0.45	0.16
	FA	-0.20	0.35	0.27	0.29
	WÜ	-0.47	0.28	0.17	0.33
total		0.19	0.18	0.28	0.08

vestigated—Teacher Training College students—the intelligence structure has a surprisingly small influence upon the subjective information.
This applies irrespective of the method used to determine H_{sub}.

When parallel group tests are carried out, it is less important to match
subjects according to intelligence than according to other variables relevant to the investigation, such as previous knowledge of the subject matter
of the text, etc.

2.6   Extension of the Procedure

Mixed Repertory. The signs and supersigns used in ordinary prose
are letters and words, respectively. When we determine the subjective
information of such a text, it is permissible to neglect the small proportion
of signs which are not accounted for in the 32 characters of the branching
diagram, such as Greek letters and figures. This omission is not permissible for such texts as account books, textbooks, technical books and
scientific reports, nor for those that occur on the business and sports
pages of newspapers. Any of these texts, according to their special character,
will include a significant proportion of figures and symbols. Any statement
concerning textual information will be incomplete unless we are able to include such texts in our investigations, because they occur frequently,
particularly in educational books. In addition to the information of texts

with mixed repertories, we also have a special interest in comparing the information of non-letter signs with that of letters. It is even possible that we might be able to draw some conclusions from this work as to the readability of such texts.

In theory, all guessing procedures can be applied to any repertory of signs. However, if one attempts to apply Shannon's guessing-game method to large repertories, the difficulties which arise are almost insurmountable. For signs rich in information, the guessing tests have to be continued until the correct sign has been predicted. If the repertory contains 60 or more signs, this can prevent the test from being carried out at all. This emphasizes the basic advantage gained by introducing branching diagrams, since the addition of one more branching stage doubles the number of elements that can be considered.

By means of an extended branching diagram, we may begin by dividing the entire repertory into subrepertories. Possible subrepertories are: Greek letters, figures, mathematical symbols, chemical symbols, technical symbols, pragmatic symbols (Weltner, 1967 b).

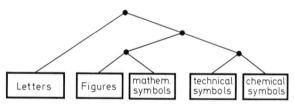

Fig. 2.21   Extended branching diagram, mixed repertory.

The branching diagram is constructed so that the subrepertory of the sign to be predicted must be guessed first at the earliest decision points. The tree continues to branch in familiar fashion inside the subrepertory until all the signs in question have been dealt with.

The subject has the extended diagram in front of him during prediction so that he no longer, as for our 32 characters, comes to the individual sign via 5 decision points, but via k decision points. The results are evaluated separately for the various subrepertories.

Example of a subrepertory with k decision points:

The result of the empirical tests is the relative proportion of incorrect predictions, N_F/N, and hence the mean information *per decision point*.

Then the mean information per symbol of the subrepertory is

$$H_{\text{sub}} = K \cdot H_{\text{dec. pt.}}(p) \qquad (2\text{--}50)$$

where $p = N_F/N$ and

$$H_{\text{dec. pt.}}(p) = \frac{1}{2}\left[p \,\text{ld}\, \frac{1}{p} + (1-p) \,\text{ld}\, \frac{1}{(1-p)} + 2p \right]. \qquad (2\text{--}51)$$

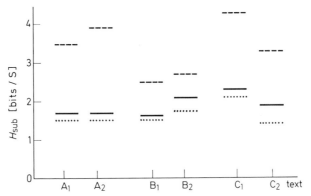

Fig. 2.22   Subjective information of mixed repertory. ---- symbols; · · · letters; —— weighted average.

If we wish to determine in addition the information of the given change of repertory, the evaluation may be carried out in greater detail by recording the results for particular decision points separately. For instance, it is possible to isolate the information related to the actual change of repertory.

The subjective information of textbooks (chemistry, arithmetic) and of the business page of a newspaper was determined empirically. The proportion of non-letter symbols in each text was about 10%.

The results are shown in Fig. 2.22.

Three values are entered above each text: bottom H_{sub} (letters), top H_{sub} (non-letters), and in between the weighted average H_{sub} (mixed repertory). For the full table of test results, see note (2/10).

On average, the subjective information of non-letter symbols in all three texts is larger than that for letters almost by a factor of two. Because the non-letter symbols make up only about 10% of the mixed text, the mean subjective information of the mixed text still falls within the range of values generally applicable to written language. The subjective information of the figures and symbols is hardly reduced at all by the preceding text. These signs depend very little on the context, and in any case less than the letters do. Texts with mixed repertories generally consist predominantly of letters. The figures and symbols scattered within them are text locations having extremely high information. We can give two reasons for this:

1. The additional information associated with the change of subrepertory;

2. The fact that the non-letter symbols depend less upon the context.

We may say that the figures and symbols represent islands of high subjective information; their consequences for textual readability in general, and for the design of textbooks in particular, will be discussed in Chapter 4.

The utility of expanding the guessing scheme lies in the fact that in theory there are no limits to the inclusion of any desired repertory. By constructing problem-oriented branching diagrams, we can determine the subjective information of texts consisting of any desired sign repertory. There is also no need to limit the number of signs, as this will not affect the use of the method. If the individual decisions are recorded in a suitable manner while the empirical tests are being carried out, it is possible to make separate determinations of the subjective information of the various sign repertories and of the information of the change of repertory. The fact of having expanded the branching scheme makes it very plain that it is here being used as a decision scheme and shows how it fixes the strategy of decision.

Such fixed decision strategies may also be built up for classes of real objects, as is done for a different purpose in the classification schemes in works on taxonomy.

The guessing games "Twenty Questions" or "17 and 4" are based upon a variable class division which has to be determined by the player. An optimal strategy, in which the player forms classes with expectation values of approximately equal probability, is found to contain elements from a repertory of some 2^{21} possibilities. Possibilities of the order of one million exceed the vocabulary of the language, so that usually the objects to be guessed consist of a sequence of words rather than a single word that always codes a single class of elements. Example: "Harold Wilson's pipe".

For mixed repertories, too, the more precise determination of the narrower limits of subjective information was carried out empirically

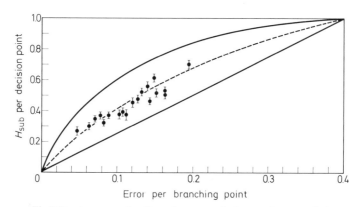

Fig. 2.23   Average value H_{sub} of narrower limits, non-letter symbols.

according to the procedure detailed in 2.5.2. The investigation was based on random samples of business news, arithmetic books and chemistry books. As with letters, the narrowed limits move closer together and approach the average value of the original limits. See Fig. 2.23 and table of test results in note (2/11).

The average-value curve from the original limits can also be assumed to be the best estimate of the true value of subjective information when dealing with sign sequences from different repertories to be predicted by means of the expanded scheme.

2.7 Simplified Procedures for Determining Subjective Information

Even though it is possible to expand the branching diagram so as to determine the subjective information of any desired repertory, and to refine the procedure so as to bound this information within narrow limits, a fundamental difficulty still remains.

This is that, when a person is reading, information uptake occurs at a considerably faster rate than in our experiments. Normal reading speed lies between 500 and 1,000 characters per minute. But the information flow rate in the guessing experiments is very much slower, being about 10 characters per minute for the normal procedure and as low as 5 characters per minute for the more exact procedure. This reduction in the information flow by nearly two orders of magnitude changes the state of mind of the recipient.

Because the subject must concentrate for a longer time on certain text passages and progresses only a letter at a time, he finds it difficult to take in the context and meaning of the text. This means that the time interval for working through text passages which stand in a logical or syntactical relationship to the preceding ones is unduly prolonged. As fully explained below in Chapter 4, the limitations of short-term memory and the narrowness of consciousness diminish the number of simultaneously known relationships which enable the subject to reduce the information. These *systematic errors* may mean that the measured subjective information is too high. Further, the emphasis on the technique of prediction, particularly when the more exact method is used, can have the effect of pushing syntactic and contextual relations that otherwise would reduce the information, right out of the subject's awareness so that he can no longer call upon them to improve his prediction.

To avoid these systematic errors, methods of increasing prediction speed must be developed so that the information flow rate during the test will approximate to that of normal reading. In addition, the experimental technique must be simplified so as to minimize the extent to which the technique itself interferes with prediction. If we succeed in speeding up the performance of the test, it will at the same time become possible to investigate larger samples of text and to reduce the sampling error relative to the complete text.

2.7.1   Simplified Procedure (1); Prediction by Letters

During prediction tests, a relationship is observed between the subjective information of a text and the proportion of signs which will be correctly predicted. The smaller the information of a text, the less uncertainty is there concerning the continuation of the sequence of signs and the less, therefore, the proportion of falsely predicted symbols. This is already clear from the results communicated by Shannon (1951) and Carson (1959). We analyzed this relationship for all our test material. We can obtain two values for each test: the subjective information per sign, and the proportion of signs falsely predicted at the first attempt. The latter value is implicitly represented in the test protocol. In Fig. 2.24 the subjective information is plotted against the proportion of letters falsely predicted at the first attempt. The values cluster fairly closely about the curve.

This relation may be used to simplify the prediction tests by recording only the fraction of signs incorrectly guessed at the first attempt.

In the simplified method the text is still predicted letter by letter, but after an incorrect guess the subject is at once told the right letter by the tester and can thus proceed to predict the next letter.

From the relative proportion of incorrectly predicted signs it is then possible to determine the subjective information of the text sample by means of the regression curve.

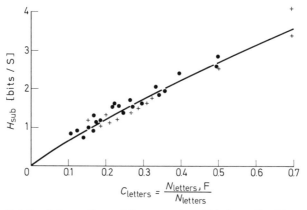

Fig. 2.24   Relation between H_{sub} and the proportion of falsely predicted letters. + college students; ● elementary school pupils.

The regression curve is slightly curved because, for theoretical reasons, it has to pass through zero, although the information can only be zero if every symbol has been correctly predicted. So for many purposes one may make use of a regressing line instead of the regression curve without introducing a significant error.

The regressing line is given by the equation:

$$H = 0.27 + 4.93 \cdot C \qquad (2\text{--}52)$$

where $C = N_F/N$.

N_F is the number of letters falsely predicted at the first attempt. The product moment correlation with H_{sub}, as determined by the more exact procedure, amounts to $r = 0.973$.

Each measured value corresponds to the prediction of on average 1,000 signs, and each data point combines the results of $8 - 12$ subjects. The average deviation of the single measurement from the compensating curve amounts to 0.07 bits. It is noteworthy that this correlation is also maintained when both texts and subjects are extremely heterogeneous. The population varies from 10-year-old schoolchildren to Teacher Training College students; the texts range from textbooks and scientific reports to programmed textbooks and narrative prose.

If we look at the regression line with a view to extrapolating it towards higher information values, we can find a point through which the curve must pass. If all 32 symbols of the repertory were equally probable and completely independent of one another, the guessing method would give an error quotient of 0.97% ($C = 0.97$) and the information of the symbols would be 5 bits. The regressing line gives the value $H = 5.04$. This value agrees so well with the theoretical one that we can assume the regressing line will hold beyond the range of points derived from empirical measurements.

The simplified method doubles the prediction rate, which rises to about 20 symbols a minute. Besides improving the subject's state of mind, this method enables text samples twice the length to be investigated in the same period of time.

2.7.2 Simplified Procedure (2); Prediction by Syllables. Simplified Procedure (3); Prediction by Words

Any further increase in prediction speed will require enlargement of the prediction unit. Syllables and words are a natural choice. Küpfmüller as long ago as 1954 used prediction tests of this kind to determine the redundancy of texts; see note (2/12).

If we can verify the hypothesis that there is a correlation between the proportion of correctly predictable syllables and words and the subjective information of the text, we can then proceed to simplify the empirical

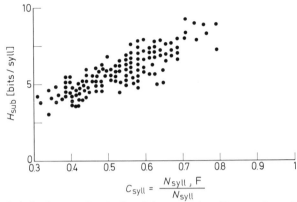

Fig. 2.25   Relation between H_{sub} (syll) and the proportion of incorrectly predicted syllables.

method still further. Using words as the unit of prediction, the procedure would be as follows:

The subject reads the beginning of the text. The text breaks off and the subject predicts the word he expects to come next. The tester either confirms the prediction or gives the correct word if the prediction was wrong. Thus the entire text sample may be predicted a word at a time. The empirical result is the relative proportion of falsely predicted words.

With text samples investigated according to the more exact method —in this connection, the simplified procedure using letters as the units of prediction is also considered a more exact procedure—we may subsequently determine the relative proportion of syllables and words for which at least one letter was incorrectly predicted. This allows us to determine the correlation between the relative proportion of incorrectly predicted words or syllables with at least one error, and the subjective

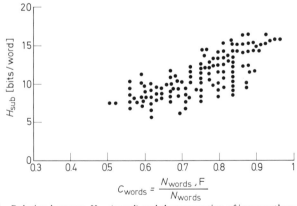

Fig. 2.26   Relation between H_{sub} (word) and the proportion of incorrectly predicted words.

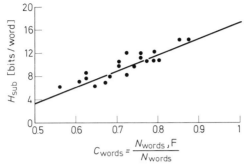

Fig. 2.27   Relation between H_{sub} (word) and the proportion of falsely predicted words; summary; regressing line.

information of the text. Fig. 2.25 shows the relation for prediction by syllables. Fig. 2.26 shows the relation for prediction by words. Each data point represents a text sample of 48 words. The product moment correlation for syllables is $r = 0.86$ and for words $r = 0.77$.

If we assume that the continuous text may be regarded as a message from an ergodic source, several samples from the same text may be combined into one.

Each composite text sample consisted of eight groups of 48 words each, predicted by 4 different subjects. The subjects revealed no differences with respect to the subjective information of the text. The result is shown in Fig. 2.27.

The variance decreases, and the product moment correlation between the subjective information of the text and the relative proportion of falsely predicted words reaches the value $r = 0.96$.

Nearly the same result is obtained for syllables, $r = 0.95$; see Weltner (1969).

This indicates the feasibility of proceeding to larger prediction units. However, this procedure must be definitively calibrated and related to the more exact determinations by means of calibration curves obtained from simultaneous experiments. These investigations will also enable us to estimate the systematic error as between the different methods. Provisional calibration curves developed by us are described in Section 5.5.

This work relates to German-language texts. The calibration curves have to be determined for each language separately. More recent work has shown that the systematic error between the various procedures is very small, and the differences between procedures were not significant.

The calibration curves given in this work have been fully confirmed.

For quite large random samples, prediction by words gives the same degree of accuracy as the procedure initially derived for prediction by

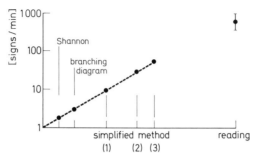

Fig. 2.28   Prediction rate for different procedures; reading speed.

syllables. The reason for this surprising finding may be that, in passing to words as units of prediction, we have reached the semantic unit in which people think. On the semantic level, the smallest unit consists of the concepts and relationships coded by words.

When words are used as units of prediction, a prediction speed of about 60 signs per minute is achieved. This is already a whole order of magnitude greater than the speed of the initial procedure, but still an order of magnitude below the speed of reading. Fig. 2.28 shows the prediction speeds of the various methods, with reading speed inserted for comparison.

The test situation may be made to approach more closely to reading conditions by careful selection of the text sample. If our text sample consists, not of sequences of words but of single words scattered over a fairly long text, with quite large segments of text between the gaps, then we can ensure that the reading process is protected to any desired extent from interference due to the prediction tests. The average speed of information uptake during reading is not much affected by isolated, scattered prediction tests, so that some 50–70 % of normal reading speed can be achieved. This statement, however, refers to the combination of information uptake from reading and guessing tests. Here, too, the word to be predicted entails an interruption.

The use of the simplified procedures increases the variance of the individual measurement; but because these procedures increase prediction speed, longer text samples may be predicted. Thus the sample error becomes smaller relative to the entire text. It is a fundamental advantage that the subject can keep context and meaning in mind so that the experimental situation is a closer approximation to the real situation of information perception during normal reading. The difficulties associated with the measurement are reduced for both subject and tester.

Test errors arising from difficulties of orientation within the branching diagrams occur more frequently with naive subjects than with college students. Measurements of subjective information for very young school-children are therefore more appropriately carried out by means of simplified procedures, unless the purpose of the experiment is to determine how information proceeds within a sentence, or to assess the information of single words or groups of words.

The exact procedures allow us to measure the information very accurately. Unfortunately, however, it puts the subject at a disadvantage: he can no longer remain aware of all the grammatical and factual clues supplied by the context which operate to reduce the information. If this situation is improved, the measuring tool becomes less exact. The simplified methods suffer from the drawback that they must always be related nomographically by means of empirically obtained calibration curves to the results of determinations which refer directly to the unit of measurement in information theory.

2.7.3   Combined Procedures: Measurement of the Subjective Information of Upper and Lower Case Letters

In the matter of spelling reform, there is some interest in the extent to which the use of upper and lower case letters assists in the identification of texts.[1] At a stroke, differentiating between capitals and small letters doubles the repertory of letters. However, since capitals occur only as the initial letters of words, the real effect of this differentiation remains far below the effect of doubling the repertory. In considering spelling reform, we must set against the gain in readability of a text due to this differentiation the amount of instructional effort required to explain and teach the rules governing the use of capitals and small letters. If we consider the question in a simplified way, neglecting the social selection mechanisms implied in the degree of mastery of this learning task, we may take the time required to learn the rules as the measure of this effort.

The student of linguistics is concerned with a particular question: How much does the fact that some classes of words begin with capital letters contribute to the information of a text? If one knows whether the next word begins with a capital or with a small letter, the repertory from which the word originates is reduced and hence the information of the word, too. The transinformation of knowing whether a word starts with a large or small letter onto the information of that word may be empirically determined.

---

[1] In German, certain classes of words are written with initial capital letters. The rules which govern this usage are complex and sometimes confusing. There are many suggestions for reforming these rules. Hence the importance of this question concerning the utility of capitalization in the identification of texts.

Our own measurements of subjective information by means of guessing-game procedures, as well as those described in the literature, have so far not distinguished between capitals and small letters. Real texts as a rule do contain capitals which vary in frequency with different languages. For instance, they are more frequent in German than in English. Therefore it may be a rewarding task, at least for printed German, to estimate the error introduced by neglecting capitals.

For the study of this special problem, we employed a combined technique, extending the branching diagram to allow separate determination of capital and small letters and using the simplified method. These experiments were set up for six fairly long text samples, and controls were used. The experimental group was asked to predict whether each new word began with a large or small letter, while the control group was not. Both groups used the simplified procedure (1) of prediction by letters. The experimental and control groups were of equal size and were matched according to the results of previous subjective information tests. During the experiment, each subject predicted according to both methods, thus minimizing the differences between the experimental and control groups.

Fig. 2.29 shows for every text: on the left H_{sub} of the control group, and on the right H_{sub} of the experimental group. Two values are given for the experimental group: the upper value is $H_{sub} = H_{capitals} + H_{letter}$ while the lower value is H_{letter}. H_{letter} is the subjective information of the letter sequence when the subject knows whether the initial letter is large or small. (see: Weltner, 1969: table in note (2/13)).

With respect to this particular problem, it was found that the effect of letter size is fairly slight for all texts investigated. When capitals are

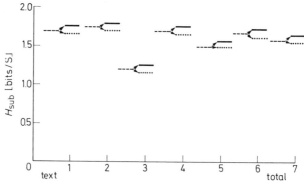

Fig. 2.29 Subjective information of upper and lower case letters. ––– Subjective information without knowledge of small and capital letters; —— subjective information with knowledge of small and capital letters; · · · subjective information when initial letter is known to be large or small.

taken into account, all texts have a few percent more subjective information, on average, about 3% more than the original value. Thus the neglect of capitals in prediction tests with German texts does not invalidate the results. This is particularly true when capital letters are disregarded in all tests, since it is the relative differences in subjective information which are of interest rather than their absolute values, and the former are not affected by the neglect of capital letters.

The subjective information for the experimental group may be divided into two parts: first, the information contained in large or small initial letters; second, the information of the letter sequence itself. If knowing whether the next word within a given context begins with a capital or small letter provides information about the word, then the subjective information of the letter sequence must be lower than in tests where no distinction is made between capital and small letters. If we compare the subjective information of a letter sequence for the experimental group and for the control group, we find that the experimental group indeed has a somewhat lower value for subjective information. The transinformation of the knowledge of capitals onto this word is, however, slight.

From the viewpoint of information theory, the extent to which differentiation between upper and lower case letters affects the subjective information of a text is of only minor interest. From the point of view of educational theory, it is also expedient to ask whether the learning time required to assimilate the rules concerning capitilization and their exceptions can be justified in view of the very slight importance of these refinements for the information of the text.

3　Transinformation Analysis

3.1　The Basic Concept of Transinformation Analysis

Our measurements of the subjective information of texts including non-letter sign sequences have generated a procedure for measuring the subjective information of the verbal formulation of complex topics. To be able to describe in terms of information theory educational processes and changes in the state of mind of pupils which can occur as a consequence of teaching, we must be able to answer certain questions.

1. In teacher-pupil communication, only some of the information imparted by the teacher is correctly received by the pupil. At best, this information is equal to, but as a rule it is less than the information transmitted. How large a proportion is it? We must further assume in our quantitative evaluation that teacher and pupil are drawing exclusively on the stock of signs which they have in common. We ask this question first with reference to spoken or written communication, but we can extend it to the information sources employed as teaching aids (pictures, experimental apparatus, films etc.)

2. The information flow consists of signs and their meanings. Hence, we must ask: How large is the proportion correctly received by the pupil in terms of meanings? The fact that the signs are correctly received is no guarantee that the meaning has been correctly perceived in the sense intended by the sender. The assumption that sender and recipient share the same stock of signs represents a rather strong constraint when information flow at the semantic level is also taken into account. We have to assume that the relationships between signs and their meanings are identical for teacher and pupils.

Thus, we have to find out what proportion of the semantic information is transferred in the communication during teaching and study the variables upon which this depends.

3. Information must not only be correctly received by the pupil, it must also be processed. Applying information theory, and in agreement with Frank (1962) and von Cube (1965), we consider for the time being that it is that part of the process of learning which can be described as a reduction on the part of the recipient of the information flowing in from the field of perception. In any event, the object of the pupil's learning must be to

reduce the information contained in future fields of perception. Frank and von Cube distinguish three processes in learning:

a) Storage—learning by rote

b) Informational accommodation = learning probability. Adapting the subjective expectation values to the objective probabilities of a field of perception reduces its information.

c) Formation of supersigns. This process involves the formation of new signs with less information by *forming categories* (generalization of concepts, statements and methods) and by *forming complexes* (combination of previously unrelated elements into new units and concepts with less information).

Extending this concept, the formation of supersigns also includes the construction of rules and methods which, when applied to perception and problem fields, lose some or all of their subjective information.

4. If, like Steinbuch (1960) and Zemanek (1961), we consider learning processes as the continuous construction by the recipient of internal models of the external world—see note (3/1)—we can formulate the question more precisely: What transinformation do these models have onto perception and problem fields? This involves the quantitative investigation of the extent to which the information of fields of events is reduced by knowledge, concepts, relationships and rules. The observable amount of transinformation from internal models onto perception fields of the external world is the effect such models have; we may draw inferences from it about the models, but it is not the same as the internal models.

Problems of this sort have already been formally presented in the section on transinformation. There we considered two event fields, stochastically dependent upon one another in varying degrees. The information of the product field equals the sum of the information of the event fields only in the special case of stochastic independence. In the case of stochastic dependence, field X already contains information regarding field Y. Hence the information of the product field is less:

$$H(XY) = H(X) + H(Y) - T(XY). \qquad (1-23)$$

The information of the product field equals the sum of the information of the stochastically dependent fields, less the transinformation of the fields onto one another.

Because of the symmetry of this relation, the transinformation is also at the same time that of field Y onto field X. It is now possible to state the questions asked above in a more precise form.

We are concerned with

1. The transinformation from the field of the message transmitted by the teacher onto the message received by the pupil.

2. The transinformation of the meaning and content intended by the teacher onto the meaning and content received by the pupil.

3. The construction of internal models of various structures and the transinformation from teaching or fields of perception onto this construction.

4. The transinformation of internal models (knowledge, rules, concepts and relationships) onto problem fields and event fields of the external world.

Let us give an example of this process. A pupil is set the following problem in a physics class: to determine by appropriate measurements whether a black box with two terminals holds one condenser, one coil, a parallel circuit of capacitor and coil, or a series circuit of condenser and coil. The event field Y contains four possible events: coil, condenser, parallel circuit, series circuit. If nothing else is known, all four events have equal probability and therefore $p=0.25$. The mean information of the event field is $H_1 = \mathrm{ld}\, 4 = 2$. The pupil has access to appropriate experimental material. The information of an event field may be reduced by a message. Suppose that the teacher, to make the task easier for the pupil, says: "There is no single condenser in the box." The transinformation of this message onto the event field can be stated directly:

One possibility has been eliminated; three possibilities remain. The conditional information of the field, assuming there is no single condenser in the box, is equal to $\mathrm{ld}\, 3 = 1.58$. Therefore the transinformation of the teacher's message M onto the event field is equal to

$$T(\mathrm{M}\,Y) = H(Y) - H(Y|\mathrm{M}) = 2.0 - 1.58 = 0.42 \text{ bit.}$$

The information that remains is

$$H_2(Y) = H(Y|\mathrm{M}).$$

The information of the event field may be further reduced by an *experiment*.

The pupil proceeds to experiment. He checks the resistance of the black box by connecting it to an oscillation generator, which measures both current and voltage. He discovers that the resistance in his box depends on the frequency of the voltage supply. Starting at the lowest value, he raises his generator frequency and observes a continuous decline in resistance up to 1,000 Hz, after which the resistance increases with increasing frequency. Which circuit is in the black box? Two boundary cases may be imagined.

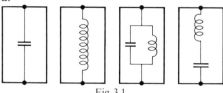

Fig. 3.1

Case A. The student knows that *only* a series circuit of condenser and coil will give minimum impedance at the resonance frequency. For him, the problem is solved with the result of measurement X. Because of his measurement, he knows it is a series circuit. For a known measured result, no uncertainty remains.

$$H(Y|X)=0$$

The transinformation of measurement X onto event field Y is equal to the mean information of the event field.

Since
$$H(Y|X)=0,$$
$$T(XY)=H_2(Y)-H(Y|X)=H_2(Y).$$

Thus two successive transinformations have reduced the entire uncertainty of the initial field to zero. The first was the transinformation of an external message M onto the event field Y, and the latter was the transinformation of experiment X onto event field Y.

Case B. The pupil does *not* know the relationship between the impedance of coils and condensers, or combinations of them, and frequency. The measurement cannot dispel his uncertainty as to the contents of the black box. If he does not know how to relate the measured result to the problem, the result is of no use to him. In this case the transinformation of the measurement onto the event field is zero. This would also be the case for a reader with no knowledge of electrical engineering. The information of the event field cannot be reduced by an experiment unless the relationship between the outcome of the experiment and the events is known. This knowledge is an internal characteristic of the pupil.

Without a knowledge of the relationships, the event field Y and the field of experimental results X are independent fields. The mean information of the product field P will then be

$$H(P)=H(XY)=H(X)+H(Y).$$

In our example with 3 events and 3 experimental results:
$$H(P)=H(XY)=H(X)+H(Y),$$
$$H(P)=1.58+1.58=3.16 \text{ bits}.$$

Given a knowledge K of the relationships, the mean information of the product field in our example is

$$H(P|K)=1.58 \text{ bits}.$$

Thus, knowledge of the relationships has reduced the information of the product field. The transinformation of the knowledge K onto the product field P is

$$T(KP)=H(P)-H(P|K)=H(X)=H(Y).$$

In our example, T (KP)=1.58 bits.

The transinformation from the internal model, that is, the relationships known to the recipient, onto the product field, consisting of experimental results and events, first reduces the information of the product field. Only after that can the remaining uncertainty be removed by experiment. In our example the information of the product field was 3.16 bits, the transinformation from the internal model onto the product field was 1.58 bits, and the transinformation from the experimental result onto the product field was also 1.58 bits.

This example makes very clear the key role played by the internal models of an individual in the reduction of the information of any field. Only if it is tacitly assumed that the relationships between experimental results and event field are known can we simplify by saying that the transinformation of the measurement onto the event field will remove the remaining uncertainty. Often, however, what concerns us most is the knowledge and abilities people possess, or which have to be cultivated, and hence their transinformation onto product fields.

Bongard (1966) and Itelson (1967) provide similar examples; they represent the special case of idealized and straightforward conditions. As a rule, however, teaching processes involve complex problems and event fields which are in addition coded in speech form. However, this problem, too, can be solved if we can measure the subjective information of verbal messages. Instead of computing the information of event fields on the assumption that these are completely defined, we must determine empirically the subjective information of messages transmitted in verbal form. In this way we can develop a method to ascertain the transinformation of verbal messages onto event fields. The subjective information of the event field must be measured for two different sets of conditions: "Message known" and "Message not known". We calculate the transinformation from the difference; see note (3/2).

This breakdown of the subjective information of the event field into single components is called *transinformation analysis*. The formal procedure for obtaining the difference is always the same, but the interpretation depends on the design of the experiment and the variables studied; see Weltner (1964 b).

The methodology of transinformation analysis may be formulated in general terms as follows:

The transinformation of a field X onto a field Y is to be measured. X can stand for either *external* fields, like messages, experimental results, perceptions, or *internal* fields, like rules, concepts and strategies which are known and understood, or facts stored in the memory. Y may also represent a similar diversity of fields. Then

$$T(XY) = H(Y) - H(Y|X). \qquad (3\text{--}1)$$

The two values on the right are observable variables. From this difference of observable values we obtain another observable value which is the transinformation. *Transinformation analysis* allows a large number of problems relevant to education to be investigated empirically. Examples are given in the following sections.

3.2   Didactic Transinformation

The information-theory correlate of such educational concepts as subject matter and teaching objectives is raised to the semantic level. A differentiated taxonomy like Bloom's (1956) is established for attainable educational objectives, so giving a coded classification of educational goals.

A rough differentiation might be knowledge on the one hand and operationally defined objectives on the other.

These teaching goals are not independent of one another. Knowledge of facts, relationships, laws, and concepts is essential to operationally defined objectives like performing mathematical or logical operations, analyzing certain classes of problems, constructively solving certain types of tasks, or applying rules. In the definitions of subject matter and teaching objectives according to Klafki's theory of category formation (1963), or Wagenschein's concept of paradigmatic teaching and learning (1962), educational goals are also for the most part operationally defined. Both regard transference as the objective of teaching, i.e. the ability to transfer to new problem situations insights into the structure of representative classes of objects and the methods appropriate thereto. It is precisely here that the constraints which regulate the transfer of any given category system to the domain of definition make themselves felt. Education must achieve its aims by treating subject matter taken from the classes of objects which are to be opened up by working on them.

We may note that it is a characteristic common to all general definitions of teaching objectives that the intake and processing of the subject matter is seen as either a transitional stage or the final goal of the teaching and learning process. The subject matter in practical teaching consists of textbooks, source material, and sets of exercises. Unlike the teaching objectives in laboratory learning experiments or experiments with animals, the usual subject matter of teaching is processed extracts from highly complex and by no means contradiction-free systems of human knowledge and societal norms. The extracts themselves represent intrinsically complex systems of statements, definitions, equations, and relationships. The concrete task before us is to measure the information content of any given subject matter. This might be, for instance:

the operation of an electric motor;
the life history of the salmon;
the content of the Potsdam agreement.

The information of the subject matter will be called *didactic information*. If this didactic information can be expressed in units of information, it is then possible to derive directly from this a measure of the rate of information flow during an instructional procedure or when working through a teaching program. When the subject matter is presented in verbalized form, e.g. in a textbook, the subjective information can be tailored to suit a certain audience or group of pupils. A textbook which presents the entire content of a given field of instruction without any redundancy will be called a *basic text*. Several constraints must be placed upon the formulation of the basic text, and these will be discussed below. Suffice it to say that the basic text should cover the content of its subject field completely and concisely and be formulated so as to be understood by its potential users.

If the user already has the appropriate mental equipment which is normally striven for during teaching, he could use the basic text for private study and so acquire all the necessary subject knowledge. So if we measure the subjective information of a basic text, we shall obtain a value which includes the didactic information.

We carried out an investigation to determine the subjective information that a basic text on the four-stroke engine has for users of different age groups in a Realschule[2].

Grades: 5—10
Length of basic text: 5,050 characters
Test group per class: 12 children
Text sample per child: four sequences of three words,
each sequence selected at random.

The sample of 12 children was selected so as to be representative of each class in regard to the range of grades in German and mathematics. The same text sample was assigned to children of equivalent school achievement. The remainder of the class, which also represented a selected sample but of $N = 12$ to 18, worked through a conventional text about four-stroke engines. The test was conducted by college students.

---

[2] The Realschule represents a medium grade of educational oportunity. The pupils, aged roughly 10 to 16 years, will later proceed to specific vocational training.

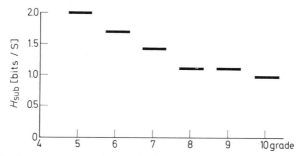

Fig. 3.2   Subjective information of a basic text as function of length of schooling.

As Fig. 3.2 shows, the subjective information of a basic text is a function of length of schooling. The information decreases with increasing school age, which indicates that the older classes have a better command of the subject matter; this must therefore reduce the didactic information. The curriculum provides for the 4-stroke engine to be covered in the 7th or 8th grade.

The prediction method involving the use of branching diagrams was used to determine the subjective information; however, the children were always encouraged to give sensible continuations to the word repertory. The word sequence is restricted for the percipient subject by the meanings he associates with each word and by the known or unknown relations which exist between these meanings. The subject matter is defined on the level of meanings and relations, that is, on the semantic level. Measuring the subjective information in the basic text will certainly pick up the information on the semantic level. There is, however, included in this globally measured information a further component, which is independent of the actual subject matter. The following considerations will make it clear (Weltner, 1964) that the information of the basic text must contain other information components in addition to the didactic information.

A given subject content does not imply any particular attitude to its verbal presentation. Any given subject may be set out in a large number of different ways, such as breaking it down into paragraphs and formulating the sentences in various styles, so as to produce a number of formally different basic texts which will nevertheless have the same subject content. Because the relationship between subject content and verbal encoding is fluid, the degrees of freedom in the formulation of a given subject content generate uncertainty about the actual formulation chosen by the author of the basic text. This uncertainty concerning the formulation possesses an information component which we will call the *aesthetic information* of the basic text; see Frank (1966); Weltner (1966) and note (3/3).

In order to determine the didactic information, we must also measure the aesthetic information. It can then be subtracted from the total information of the basic text, leaving the didactic information as the difference.

The following considerations are relevant to determining the aesthetic information:

For a subject expert, the basic text contains no didactic information. He cannot learn anything new from the basic text. All that it contains for him is aesthetic information, that is, the information of its actual formulation. The expert has long since received and mastered the didactic information. So, for him, the information in the sequence of signs is the total information less the didactic information, because he draws from the knowledge of meanings and relations that he has within him the transinformation that reduces the information of the basic text to the aesthetic component.

We can measure the aesthetic information of the basic text by determining the subjective information of the text for pupils who already know the subject matter in question.

We carried out empirical investigations as follows:

The pupils in the classes participating in the experiment worked through a teaching program covering the 4-stroke engine. The use of programmed teaching material facilitated the empirical research on the teaching process, since the lesson used was standardized and to a large extent reproducible in identical form. This approach appreciably reduces the variance due to differences in teacher attitudes. After working through the program, the children should have had available to them all the subject knowledge contained in the basic text and hence should have become experts. The measurement of the subjective information of the basic text for these presumably expert children was carried out three days after they had finished working on the teaching program. The programmed text for the 4-stroke engine is a linear program and the version used in the experiment comprised 244 frames. The study time amounted to 3 to 4 hours of instruction. Care was taken during the conduct of the experiment to see that no child at any time saw a text passage whose subjective information was to be determined later on. The control groups were again given a conventional achievement test which was identical to the preliminary test.

The results are shown in Fig. 3.3; see also note (3/5).

With the exception of the 5th grade, for whom the program was too difficult, the subjective information of all groups fell to the more or less constant value of 0.9 bits per symbol. There are no significant differences between grades. It is this remaining information for grades 6 − 10 which is the measure of the aesthetic information in the basic text. If we now subtract the aesthetic information from the initial subjective information,

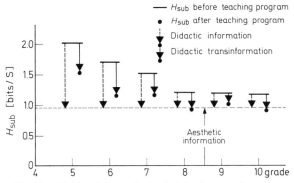

Fig. 3.3   Didactic information and didactic transinformation.

the difference is the didactic information of the basic text. The didactic information is a function of school age.

The didactic information provides us with a unit of measurement in accordance with information theory which allows us to express the content of the subject matter quantitatively. Theoretically, this enables us to estimate the didactic information of any given subject for any given group of users.

Transinformation analysis for each grade yields the difference in the subjective information of the basic text before and after the study process, i.e. the *didactic transinformation*, which is the information actually transferred as a result of the study process. The didactic transinformation is a unit of measurement in accordance with information theory which measures the learning increment: T (teaching, basic text) = H (basic text) − H (basic text|teaching). In our experiment, for grades 6 − 10 the didactic transinformation and the didactic information of the basic text are identical. In grade 5, only some of the didactic information is transferred as didactic transinformation. Even after working through the teaching program, the pupils of grade 5 are still not experts.

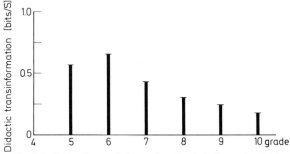

Fig. 3.4   Didactic transinformation, Realschule, grades 5–10.

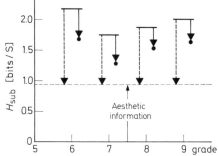

Fig. 3.5   Didactic information, didactic transinformation, Volksschule, grades 6–9.

Fig. 3.4 shows the didactic transinformation for each grade. It has a maximum for grade 6 and a minimum for grade 10. The reason is trivial: the children were already familiar with the subject matter prior to working through this teaching program; see note (3/4).

A similar experiment was carried out in four Volksschule classes[3]; the results are summarized in Fig. 3.5. The dotted line indicates the value of the aesthetic information; for table of results, see note (3/5). The didactic information was higher for the groups participating in this experiment. In all groups the didactic transinformation on working through the teaching program was less than the didactic information of the basic text.

The program for Volksschule children was changed after this. For pupils of the 6th grade prior to instruction, the subjective information of the basic text—as measured by Weltner (1964)—gave values comparable to those obtained in other experiments with scrambled texts. For these children, the basic text is not immediately comprehensible, so that there is no proper basis here for determining the didactic information.

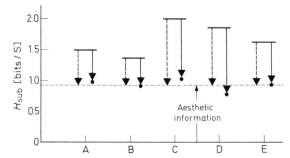

Fig. 3.6   Didactic information, didactic transinformation, basic text: "Flip-flop shift re-
gisters". A university students, B technical-college students, C and D high-school
students, E engineering students.

---

[3] The children in the Volksschule were comparable in age. They represent, however, a non-
-selected school population who will probably become manual workers on leaving school.

Rauner and Krumme (1967) undertook an experiment along the same lines with a teaching program on the "Fundamentals of Data Processing", administered to heterogeneous user groups composed of high-school students, engineering students, university students and technical-college students.

Here, too, the basic text contained a varying amount of subjective information for the different groups before they worked through the teaching program; afterwards the subjective information declined for all groups to the constant value of 0.95 bit per sign; see Fig. 3.6 and note (3/6).

These experiments were independent, and both sets yielded a value of about 0.9 bit per typewriter stroke for the aesthetic information. Frank (1969) points out that a lower value of aesthetic information is found for mathematical basic texts, namely about 0.6 bits per typewriter stroke. This is understandable because, with mathematical textbooks in particular, the degrees of freedom in formulation are restricted, and there is an appreciable use of stereotypes in the text passages linking the various mathematical operations.

These experiments have demonstrated the theoretical possiblity of expressing the subject content of a lesson or a lecture in the units of measurement of information theory, and of making statements about the semantic information content. If we take the duration of the instruction into account, we can compute the rate of information flow. For the experiments discussed, the didactic transinformation within an instruction period is of the order of magnitude of 600 to 1,300 bits per lesson (45 minutes) or 0.2 to 0.5 bits per second. Note that, as the didactic transinformation was determined three days after the course was concluded and the study program lasted from three to five days, these values refer to memory inputs on average five days old.

3.2.1   Correlation between the Subjective Information of the Basic Text and Achievement Tests Related to the Teaching Program

In all experiments, the teaching success of the programmed instruction was determined on parallel groups by means of normal achievement tests specially developed for each particular program.

Fig. 3.7 shows the relation between the subjective information of the basic text and the percentage of correct answers in the achievement tests. The correlation of the measured values,

$$r = -0.88,$$

is so high that the agreement between the determination of subject knowledge according to information theory and the relative value of the points

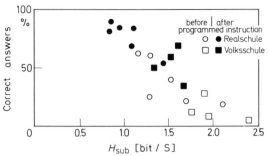

Fig.3.7   Correlation between H_{sub} (basic text) and informal achievement tests.

awarded in the achievement test certainly indicates that we are proceeding along the right lines. In the experiment carried out by Rauner and Krumme (1967), too, an informal test on the program correlated highly with the subjective information:

$$\text{rank correlation} = -0.80.$$

We may take it as proved that learning increments can be measured by a method based on information theory because of the good agreement obtained with the relative learning increment as assessed by achievement tests. This suggests that it may be possible to equate the more easily applied procedure of measuring achievement to the unit of measurement of information theory. The latter, though more difficult to handle, rests upon a more exact foundation.

The subjective information of a basic text is a measure which enables us to estimate the content of *one* body of instructional material for a *number* of user groups. The greater the content of the subject matter, the more didactic information it holds, and the less advisable it appears to use only one teaching program to transfer all the didactic information. Certainly, time adaptivity, that is, the subjective variation of the speed of working, offers a means of matching the duration of the learning process to the

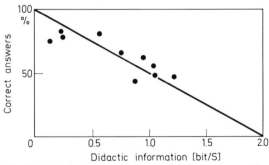

Fig.3.8   Relationship between didactic information and final test.

amount of didactic information, but there are limits to such adaptivity. The success of the teaching program can be forecast *before* working through the teaching program on the basis of the didactic information of the basic text. A fairly close relationship is found between the scores in the final test and the didactic information of the basic text; see Fig. 3.8. In other words, the outcome of the final test is inversely proportional to the amount of didactic information.

The product-moment correlation is

$$r = -0.94; \qquad N = 10 \text{ groups.}$$

Frank inferred from this that, when the didactic information of the basic text is known, the length of the required teaching-program text can be estimated. Such a procedure could be based on the values investigated by Riedel (1967) concerning the age dependence of informational and psychological parameters. The model of psychological structure presented by Frank and Riedel shows a clear relationship between the didactic information, the age-dependent parameters, the length of the teaching steps, and the length of the teaching program. This relationship can be developed logically for working out values for repetition and exercises in the algorithmic generation of teaching programs.

Summary. The application of transinformation analysis to textbook-type presentations of subject matter (basic texts) enables the didactic information of a subject to be determined empirically as the transinformation onto the basic text of the knowledge which an expert has within him.

The didactic transinformation is the transinformation on to the basic text of the changes in the internal state induced by teaching. The empirical determination also takes account of the changes which occur between time t_1 (end of instruction) and t_2 (measurement).

$$T(\text{teaching, basic text}) = H(\text{basic text}) - H(\text{basic text}|\text{instruction}).$$

3.2.2 Iteration Procedure for Complete Determination of the Didactic Information

Determining the didactic information with the aid of a basic text requires various assumptions which may be formulated as requirements upon the basic text. For instance, "the basic text must be concise, but written so that the potential user can understand it". To be precise, the subjective information of the basic text must not exceed 1.8 bits/symbol. A more stringent and exact requirement upon the basic text is that all concepts and relations which are new to the reader must be explained in the text. Hence, new concepts and relations may not be used in the text, until they have been explained. The reason for this requirement is obvious, but checking for it is not trivial.

First there must be a logical analysis of the basic text to identify concepts and relations which are assumed but not explained in the basic text. Such an analysis has been carried out by Lansky (1969); it can also be done by means of the *coherence structure diagram* borrowed from network theory, as described in Section 4.4. This gives a number, V, of assumed concepts and relations—Lansky calls them supporting concepts —and the assumption that they are already known to the reader must be checked in every case.

This checking can be done empirically by means of transinformation analysis. The transinformation of the concept is measured from a definition of the concept. The definition or explanation of the concept must define it exactly as used in the context of the basic text. If a concept can be employed at more than one level of abstraction, it is the level deduced from its application in the basic text which must be used. If the concept so defined is subjectively known, the subjective information of the explanation will sink to the level of aesthetic information. Then the transinformation of the internally known concept onto this explanation is equal to the didactic information of the explanation of the concept. We might also say that the concept is fully known when the didactic information of the explanation approaches zero.

Let the basic text contain a finite number r_1 of such concepts. Let there be one explanation for each concept. For the expert, let this explanation have the aesthetic information $I_j^{(1)}$ (expert); for the user let the explanation have the subjective information $I_j^{(1)}$ (user). Then the concept j will have the didactic information

$$I_D^{(1)}j = I_j^{(1)} (user) - I_j^{(1)} (expert). \qquad (3-2)$$

Thus $I_{Dj}^{(1)}$ is an empirically observable magnitude.

A basic text in which concepts or relations have been used with didactic information $I_{Dj}^{(1)}$ which does not vanish for all j's (for the user) without their having been explained or defined within the basic text, is an *incomplete basic text*. An incomplete basic text does not meet the requirement stated above for the measurement of the didactic information of the subject matter. An incomplete basic text must be supplemented by a first-stage auxiliary basic text which contains explanations and definitions for concepts and relations whose didactic information $I_{Dj}^{(1)}$ did not approach zero. The didactic information of the first-stage auxiliary basic text is then

$$I_D^{(1)} = \sum_{j=1}^{r_1} I_{Dj}^{(1)}. \qquad (3-3)$$

If $I_D^{(0)}$ is the didactic information of the incomplete basic text, then the complete didactic information of the basic text will be

$$I_D = I_D^{(0)} + I_D^{(1)}. \qquad (3\text{–}4)$$

If a basic text used as the basis of instruction or for the development of a teaching program is incomplete, an additional preparatory learning phase must be introduced. The complete didactic information of the subject matter therefore exceeds that of the incomplete basic text by the amount of the didactic information of the explanations and definitions given in the first-stage auxiliary text. It is always an indication that a basic text is incomplete when, during measurement of the subjective information, supporting concepts have a very high information value. It is also apparent when such concepts must be predicted letter by letter to the very end, and the subject fails to make any intelligent deductions from the context. Logical analysis must also be applied to the first-stage auxiliary basic text, since it too necessarily contains concepts and relations which are assumed to be known. Let the auxiliary basic text contain a finite number r_2 of such concepts; then by analogy the didactic information of those concepts is

$$I_D^{(2)} = \sum_{j=1}^{r_2} I_{Dj}^{(2)}. \qquad (3\text{–}5)$$

Unless all the terms on the right approach zero, this will be an incomplete first-stage auxiliary basic text and it will have to be supplemented by a *second-stage* auxiliary basic text. Now the didactic information of the subject matter is given by

$$I_D = I_D^{(0)} + I_D^{(1)} + I_D^{(2)}. \qquad (3\text{–}6)$$

Thus we build up an iteration procedure by means of which the user's normal language and concept repertory can be identified via any desired number of stages. The complete didactic information of the subject matter is therefore that of the basic text plus the sum of the didactic information of all supporting concepts and relations over all stages s,

$$I = \sum_{k=0}^{s} I^{(k)} \qquad (3\text{–}7)$$

or, in more detail,

$$I = \sum_{k=1}^{s} \sum_{j=1}^{r_k} I_j^{(k)}. \qquad (3\text{–}8)$$

The terms on the right-hand side represent the didactic information of the supporting concepts. Their number increases extremely rapidly when higher stages are included in s; the contributions from higher stages will not rapidly approach zero until the didactic information of the auxi-

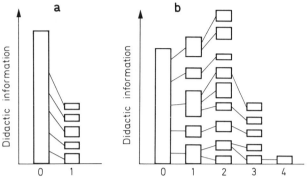

Fig. 3.9 Increase in didactic information when incomplete basic texts must be supplemented by auxiliary basic texts. a first stage auxiliary basic text; b auxiliary basic texts, stages 1–4.

liary concepts and relations differs from zero only for small s. It is a direct consequence of this that a basic text cannot be taken as the basis of instruction or of teaching-program texts unless the didactic information of the auxiliary concepts is of the same order of magnitude as that of the basic text. The auxiliary basic text must meet this requirement before it can be integrated into the teaching. This can be done for teaching-program texts by branching techniques or in lessons by introducing explanations from the auxiliary basic text.

If first-stage supporting concepts have didactic information which is not zero, the sum of these can easily attain values considerably above those of the incomplete basic text; see Fig. 3.9. Where this is the case, a new strategy of instruction must be devised. This should comprise the total didactic information and its interrelations as seen in a coherence structure diagram.

Let us take an extreme case: if our incomplete basic text is the final chapter of an instruction to the theory of relativity, the iteration procedure will construct auxiliary basic texts at successive stages until it has generated a complete introduction to the theory of relativity.

Though the method is cumbersome in execution, it does show that it is in principle possible to measure the total didactic information of quite difficult and complex subjects. It is clear that the didactic information may attain high values for coherent subjects with, say, a mathematical or physical content, where a broad conceptual system is involved. This system must be built up so as to link the user's preliminary knowledge, which may be of any degree of incompleteness, with the knowledge required to enable him to understand the basic text.

The iteration method also reveals how large can be the didactic information of relatively short abbreviations found in basic texts. When such abbreviations are unknown, their contribution to the didactic information is small if the measurement is based on the incomplete basic text. The full amount of their contribution only becomes apparent when the iteration process is carried out.

The logical analysis of basic texts, which must be done before the iteration process can be applied, has up to the present been most thoroughly performed by Lansky (1969) in his investigations relating to the Anschütz diagram and Zifreund's structural-analytical diagram. Lansky is here studying the position of concepts within complex systems of concepts and relationships. He distinguishes between concepts explained in the text (explanandum) and concepts used in explaining them (explanans or supporting concepts). Lansky then arranges within a conceptual framework the explanations (by which he understands the incomplete definitions, in the sense of formal logic) of the concepts to be learned by means of the supposedly known supporting concepts. In so doing, he proceeds directly from the repertory of semantic concepts relevant to the process of education and describes their structure and how they may be built up by teaching programs. Our method of measuring the complete didactic information by means of the iteration procedure creates a link with the empirically measurable amount of subjective information in these concepts.

3.3   Semantic Transinformation

3.3.1   Synonyms; Semantic Potential

Information theory was applied directly without any particular difficulty to syntactical sign sequences, since these are accessible to statistical treatment. However, fundamental difficulties arose in applying information theory to semantic information, which is what is of chief interest in education. In dealing with such complex subject matter as is found in teaching material, it has proved possible to adapt the methods of information theory to the semantic level. Didactic information and didactic transinformation were defined initially on the semantic level. Furthermore, transinformation analysis may be applied to the study of semantic units such as ideas and concepts and where they agree and disagree.

Words are signs and, as such, are carriers of meaning. The word STREET has the same meaning as the word STRASSE, but the first belongs to the repertory of the English language, the other to German. Within the same language, too, different signs may have the same meaning.

Synonyms: STREET and ROAD.

Let us assume two signs which have the same meaning. If one of the signs is called, the meaning is hereby defined. If we then call a second sign having the same meaning, its information will be zero, assuming that the subject is familiar with both the words which have the same meaning: STREET and ROAD. This relation may be verified empirically by determining the subjective information of a word known to have the same meaning as STREET. The subjective information of the word ROAD approaches zero.

That different signs possess identical meaning is a limiting case. It is usually the case with synonyms that the complex of meanings of concept A is not entirely identical with that of concept B. The two concepts have an area of intersection within which their meanings overlap. One concept may have several synonyms B_j and the areas of intersection of their meanings do not necessarily coincide. Now, where the transinformation of a concept onto its synonyms is determined, it is possible to use transinformation analysis to find the extent of the areas of intersection, in other words, how much information they have in common. This was shown by Rollet (1969).

Experimental procedure:

Subjects in Group I are given a concept A. The subjective information of concepts B_j, which are synonymous with A, is then determined. The subjects know that the concepts B_j which they are to predict are synonyms of A.

Group II subjects are tested for the subjective information of the same concepts in random order, that is, in a scrambled text. Both groups know the word category to which the synonyms belong. The situation of the two groups in the experiment differs only on the semantic level. The reduction of the subjective information of the synonyms is the transinformation of the meaning of the known concept onto the synonymous concepts. This semantic transinformation is

$$t(AB_j) = i(B_j) - i(B_j|A). \tag{3–9}$$

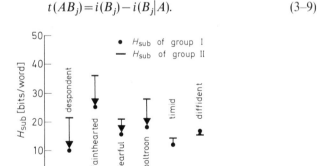

Fig. 3.10   Semantic transinformation, synonyms for "cowardly".

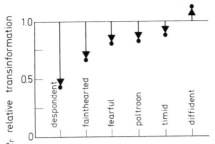

Fig. 3.11   Relative semantic transinformation, synonyms.

The transinformation is here determined for elements and not for fields; hence it is not the mean information H, but rather the information i of the elements which is used. Rollet (1969) carried out empirical measurements on the students of the Osnabrück Teacher Training College. A computer was used to facilitate the prediction tests; see Heinrich/Weltner (1969).

Fig. 3.10 shows for the given concept the subjective information of various synonyms for Groups I and II. The difference is the semantic transinformation.

Fig. 3.11 presents the relative semantic transinformation referred to unity; i.e. the fraction of the transinformation relative to the information of the given concept A:

$$t_{\mathbf{R}}(AB_j) = \frac{i(B_j) - i(B_j|A)}{i(B_j)}. \qquad (3\text{--}10)$$

Strictly speaking, we are dealing with two combined transinformations: the transinformation of meaning A into meaning B_j, and that of meaning B_j into sign B_j.

The synonyms are arranged in order of decreasing semantic transinformation. The smaller the semantic transinformation, the less the amount of meaning two concepts have in common and hence the larger the area of meaning each concept possesses which is foreign to the other. Let us call this arrangement of synonyms in order of decreasing semantic transinformation or increasing independence of each other the *semantic potential*. For concepts which are not synonyms, that is, those which have no meaning in common with the anchor concept, the semantic transinformation must approach zero. In the empirical experiments the semantic transinformation is generally negative, in other words, a concept which is not a synonym has more information for Group I, the experimental group, than for Group II, the control group. This is understandable, since subjects in Group I were informed in advance that the concepts B_j were synonyms of A. Hence, for them, the probability that a concept

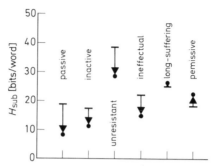

Fig. 3.12   Semantic transinformation, antonyms to "active".

which is not a synonym will occur is less than it would have been without this advance information.

3.3.2   Semantic Transinformation for Antonyms; Semantic Differential

Transinformation analysis was applied to antonyms in the same way as to synonyms. For Group I the subjective information is measured of a cluster of concepts known in advance to be opposite in meaning to the anchor concept. For Group II the subjective information of the same cluster of concepts is determined from a scrambled text. The transinformation is then

$$t(\mathrm{non}\ A, B_j) = i(B_j) - i(B_j|\mathrm{non}\ A). \qquad (3\text{–}11)$$

Fig. 3.12 sets out the results of the empirical investigations (Rollet, 1969; Heinrich/Weltner, 1969); here the subjective information of the concept is recorded for each individual concept in the scrambled text and whether the antonym was known.

Here too, the relative transinformation can be determined in exactly the same way as the semantic transinformation:

$$t_{\mathrm{R}}(\mathrm{non}\ A, B_j) = \frac{i(B_j) - i(B_j|\mathrm{non}\ A)}{i(B_j)}. \qquad (3\text{–}12)$$

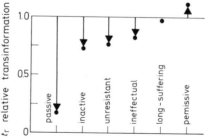

Fig. 3.13   Relative semantic transinformation, antonyms to "active"

In Fig. 3.13 the concepts are arranged in order of decreasing transinformation. The semantic potential has a similar course to that of the synonyms in Fig. 3.11. However, it should be noted that the relative transinformation of the antonym at the bottom of the scale is greater than with the synonyms. This finding is not peculiar to this particular example, it is general. For set pairs of antonyms, the semantic transinformation is significantly greater than for synonyms. Pairs of antonyms were employed by Osgood (1952) and Hofstätter (1955) in developing their polarity profile method for determining the semantic differential; their aim was to determine the position of a concept within the spectrum defined by the polarities. Such word pairs may also be studied with respect to their semantic transinformation. This still leaves the question as to whether the amount of the semantic transinformation of antonyms influences the stability of the classification.

A rank order, such as is seen in the semantic potential, may also be obtained in a manner quite independent of our procedure. The subjects

Table 3-1. Rank correlation coefficient ρ between ranking for semantic potential and ranking R based on subjective grading. t_r = relative semantic transinformation

$N=5$		synonyms					
R small	t_r	R cowardly	t_r	R rough	t_r	R liberal	t_r
1 tiny	0.10	1 poltroon	0.22	1 coarse	0.48	1 libertarian	0.68
2 slight	0.42	2 fearful	0.23	2 cracked	0.26	2 independent	
						-minded	0.48
3 scanty	0.18	3 faint-		3 harsh	0.13	3 freedom-	
		hearted	0.30			loving	0.47
4 insignifi-		4 despondent	0.54	4 bristly	0.47	4 progres-	
cant	−0.11					sive	0.15
5 miserable	0.09	5 timid	0.04	5 crinkled	0.27	5 liberated	0.17
6 lowered	0.31	6 diffident	−0.06	6 prickly	0.01	6 tolerant	−0.14
	$\rho=0.60$		$\rho=0.43$		$\rho=0.54$		$\rho=0.83$

$N=5$		antonyms					
R weak	t_r	R clear	t_r	R quiet	t_r	R active	t_r
1 strong	0.64	1 blurred	0.15	1 loud	0.67	1 passive	0.84
2 mighty	0.33	2 overcast	0.51	2 rowdy	0.62	2 incapable	0.25
3 powerful	0.57	3 unrecog-		3 noisy	0.83	3 ineffectual	0.18
		nizable	0.25				
4 herculean	−0.17	4 dim	0.04	4 resounding	0.12	4 unresistant	0.24
5 gigantic	0.35	5 dusky	−0.20	5 shrill	0.35	5 per-	
						missive	−0.06
6 significant	−0.57	6 dull	−0.01	6 audible	0.22	6 long-	
						suffering	0.0
	$\rho=0.71$		$\rho=0.89$		$\rho=0.94$		$\rho=0.89$

are asked to arrange the synonyms or antonyms of a given anchor concept in accordance with the subjective degree of overlap in meaning. The rank correlation between series obtained in this way and series used for the semantic potential is shown in Table 3-1; see also Rollett (1969).

If we consider the (usually complex) meaning of a concept, we see that it may be represented as a vector in a multidimensional space, each component of the meaning being assigned to a dimension. The semantic transinformation can then be regarded as the cartesian product of the two concepts. The application of transinformation analysis allows an empirical check on the area of intersection of meanings. Besides its practical importance for the construction of suitable antonyms for semantic differentials, this procedure is of theoretical interest because it allows the influence of meaning upon the subjective information of signs to be investigated for different semantic situations.

3.4 Transinformation in Reading Processes

Transinformation for normal, once-through reading has both a semantic and an aesthetic component. If this transinformation is measured during the reading process, one first obtains the sum of both components. The semantic transinformation might be determined separately if it were possible to form experimental groups which during the reading process would perceive only the semantic information but not the aesthetic information due to the formulation. Such experimental groups may be formed artificially by having the same subject matter presented in two texts, A and B, differing in style and construction. The reader of text A will perceive the semantic information but will not have the aesthetic information of text B.

Experimental plan. A factual text A about experiments in training dolphins was rewritten to produce a parallel text B, which was completely different in style, construction, average sentence length and vocabulary. Six experimental groups were set up according to the plan given below. The information of texts A und B can then be determined from a variety of aspects. Thus, $I(A)$ means information of text A without previous knowledge, $I(A|B)$ means information of text A when text B has been read, etc.

tested on	read		
	A	B	neither
A	$I(A|A)$	$I(A|B)$	$I(A)$
B	$I(B|A)$	$I(B|B)$	$I(B)$

The average time interval between reading and determining the subjective information was 40 minutes. The results are shown in Fig.

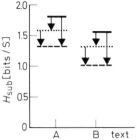

Fig. 3.14   Transinformation from reading. ——read neither text; ··· read other text; ———read own text.

3.14. The text holds the most information for the group which had read neither version. Below this is the group which had read the parallel text. The least information is measured for the group which had already read the text.

The total transinformation is

$$T(A, A) = I(A) - I(A|A) = 1750 \text{ bits,}$$

$$T(B, B) = I(B) - I(B|B) = 1720 \text{ bits.}$$

Thus the semantic transinformation is

$$T_{sem}(B, A) = I(B) - I(B|A) = 765 \text{ bits,}$$

$$T_{sem}(B, A) = I(B) - I(B|A) = 880 \text{ bits,}$$

so that the aesthetic transinformation is

$$T_{aest}(A, B) = I(A|B) - I(A|A) = 985 \text{ bits,}$$

$$T_{aest}(B, A) = I(B|A) - I(B|B) = 840 \text{ bits.}$$

Further experiments of the same kind were based on parallel texts A and B from the magazines *Die Umschau* and *Der Spiegel*. The only changes

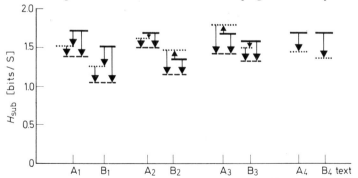

Fig. 3.15   Transinformation from reading processes. —— read neither text; ··· read other text; ——— read own text.

made involved the deletion of passages relating to matter not mentioned in the parallel text, so as to make the semantic information of both texts the same.

All the texts gave factual information about such scientific and technical topics as desalination, VTOL, and radioastronomy. The results are summarized in Fig. 3.15; see also table in note (3/7).

In two cases the transinformation is negative. This finding may be explained by the hypothesis that the semantic information of scientific and technical texts is too large for readers without appropriate education (Teacher Training College students) to construct adequate internal models on the basis of once-through reading. If part of the content is not understood or misunderstood, the part which is misunderstood may give rise to negative transinformation. This interpretation is valid only on the assumption that the semantic information of the parallel texts is the same. This condition is only approximately met. In the sense defined in section 3.2.2, the text may therefore be regarded as an incomplete basic text. Negative transinformation indicates false expectations on the part of the subjects.

In order to test this hypothesis, the reading time was increased to 30 minutes in the last experiment and at the same time the subjects were asked to study the text (5,900 signs) on radioastronomy and to write down the main divisions. The change from once-through to thorough reading increased the semantic transinformation, which then became significantly positive ($p < 0.01$).

The analysis of the transinformation during reading processes as a function of the reading technique and the structure of the text content not only provides a measure of the information received but also highlights the formation of wrong ideas.

This type of method may also be used to study the transinformation of narrative texts, advertising texts, news items, etc. A field of application of transinformation analysis which could have practical importance is the study of brochures, operating instructions, and technical explanations, relative to user groups having different levels of prior knowledge.

When reading time is taken into account and the total information flow into the memory is determined, it is found that, for the texts employed here and an average memory span of 40–60 minutes, the values are 2 to 6 bits per second.

3.5   The Semantic Information of Graphic Representations

Unlike texts, pictures are not scanned line by line by the observer but are perceived simultaneously. The static information of a text is read line by line, so that the text is resolved into a sequence of messages perceived as belonging to the repertory of letters or words. As an approximation, a text may therefore be considered as a sequence of signs. When it comes to pictures, this approximation is not even remotely valid, even though the technology of picture transmission, for instance in television, involves the resolution of the picture into dots which are transmitted in a linear sequence.

Pictorial presentation in the field of education and teaching can be considered under three aspects:

1. The picture is a work of art. Here, the interest lies in the aesthetic processes stimulated by the work of art, and in the work of art as a message from the artist within the framework of a given artistic era.

2. The picture is an objective presentation of objects, situations, configurations or persons, which cannot be observed directly.

3. The picture is a codification of some meaning which can be conveyed more concisely and clearly in graphic form, such as graphs, figures, and diagrams.

In the sense of aspects 2 and 3, pictures are lumped together in schools under the general concept "visual media". However, their function tends to be obscured rather than illuminated by the word "visual" because line drawings, sketches, and even photographs are primarily chosen for their content of relevant information. By controlled selection of the picture content, or by changing the manner of presentation of the original, the proportion of irrelevant information is suppressed so as to facilitate the process of supersign formation in the observer. In this sense, all visual aids used in schools are aids to abstraction or the formation of supersigns.

Now, the teacher is fully aware of the supersign hierarchy and the system of relationships, and it is only from his point of view that the visual media are concrete signposts on the road to perception. From the pupil's point of view, the visual media represent levels of increasing abstraction and of decreasing irrelevant information. Any consideration of these teaching aids must start out from the pupil's point of view.

If the semantic information is to be determined, transinformation analysis may be carried out in two ways:

a) The transinformation of the picture is determined from a verbal description of the content of the picture. Frank (1967) has reported the results of an empirical measurement of transinformation. With different pictures, he found appreciable differences in the transinformation of the picture onto the description of the picture. Although still not an exact measuring tool, this procedure appears capable of measuring the semantic or didactic information of pictures. In this type of measurement the subjective information of the picture is obtained only indirectly via the measurement of texts, so it is not possible to find out anything about the aesthetic information of a picture.

b) The transinformation of a description of the picture onto the picture is determined. Following the investigations of Attneave (1954, 1955), Heinrich (1969) measured the transinformation of a verbal description of a picture onto the subjective information of the picture. Attneave's experimental technique consisted in having the subjects copy a figure and extrapolate a line. Here, as in the prediction experiments with texts, the true continuation was shown afterwards. Deviations from the correct course always occurred at points where the figure contained a lot of detail, or where the line kept changing direction.

Heinrich had his pictures predicted point by point, after they had been resolved by means of a grid into 600 black and white dots. The grid used in this process must be fairly coarse because of the very large number of dots generated. Pictures of simple objects or diagrams were predicted point by point and line by line. The experimental group was always informed verbally of the picture's content whereas the control group received no information of any kind. For diagrams, the transinformation of the verbal presentation V onto the subjective information of the picture was escpecially large. For objective representations of objects, the transinformation onto the picture was surprisingly small.

Example. Elephant (Fig. 3.16)
I (picture)   :   163 bits,
I (picture$|V$)   :   156 bits,
I (V, picture) :   7 bits.

The result nevertheless is understandable if one considers that the transinformation must be of the order of magnitude of the subjective information of the content of the picture, so that, in the case of the concept *elephant*, the information is of the order of 10 bits.

With diagrams, the transinformation of the verbal presentation is larger, while the aesthetic information of the picture is smaller.

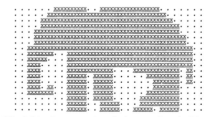

Fig.3.16   Representational picture of real object.

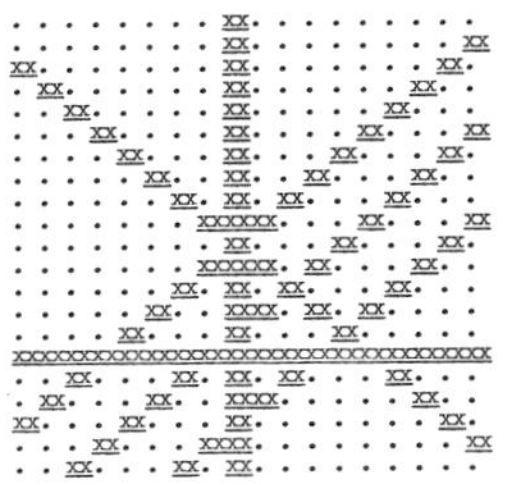

Fig. 3.17 Diagram, coordinates with straight lines.

Example. System of coordinates (Fig. 3.17)

I (picture)   : 133 bits,
I (picture$|V$) :   57 bits,
I (V, picture) :   76 bits.

The finding is in agreement with the fact that the verbal presentation of the content of the picture involves giving more information, and that diagrams are by definition media in which the amount of irrelevant aesthetic information is reduced.

3.5.1 Efficiency in Terms of Information Theory

The ratio of the didactic information of the basic text to the total information may be regarded, following Meyer-Eppler (1959) and Neidhard (1956), as its efficiency in terms of information theory

$$\eta = \frac{H(B) - H(B|\text{knowledge})}{H(B)}. \tag{3–13}$$

In normal basic texts, and probably in most textbooks, the average didactic information is about 30–50% of the total information. Thus the information-theory efficiency should be about 0.3–0.5. This figure is a function of the subject matter and reflects the fact that some subjects are easy to verbalize and others are more difficult. Mathematical basic texts contain little aesthetic information and hence may be expected to show a higher information-theory efficiency. Mathematical and scientific relations are particularly difficult to verbalize if it is desired to make precise statements without the use of mathematical symbols and formulas. In such cases the component of irrelevant information often rises so high as to interfere quite considerably with the learning process. For instance, let us assume that Ohm's law is to be expressed

1. in everyday language
2. by a diagram
3. by a mathematical formula.

The formulations will be as follows:

1. The electrical potential difference which exists within a conductor causes an electrical current to flow through it. If the potential difference increases, the current increases. The current is proportional to the potential difference, so that doubling the potential difference doubles the current.

2.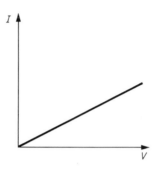

3. $R = \text{const}$, and $R = V/I$

The relevant semantic information of all three formulations is identical, but the irrelevant aesthetic information declines from formulation 1. to 3. The information-theory efficiency increases accordingly. Whenever the efficiency becomes too unsatisfactory, the purely verbal basic text must be replaced by other, more efficient forms of presentation. This involves the use of diagrams and mathematical formulae which may be thought of as abstraction aids of a high degree of efficiency in terms of information theory.

3.6   Memory Experiments

A qualitative and quantitative description of the characteristics of memory is a central issue in education, since storage in the memory is a component common to all learning processes. The extensive findings concerning memory in the psychological literature were analyzed by Riedel (1969 a) on the basis of information theory, to the extent that data were available and where the unit of information had not already been used in decribing the material; see Stevens (1965); Woodworth and Schlossberg (1954). Since transinformation analysis may equally well be applied to meaningless as to meaningful materials, it can be used without modification in memory experiments and takes its place alongside the conventional procedures of psychology; see Weltner (1967 c). The advantage of transinformation analysis is that the same principle is applied to evaluate both meaningless material to be memorized and the material which is of prime importance in education, that is, meaningful material, structured in a variety of ways.

For transinformation analysis, two parameters must be measured:

1. The subjective information $H(X)$ of the practice material X

2. the subjective information $H(X|G)$ following the memory experiment G, that is, of the practice phase and the memory span.

The difference between 1. and 2. is the transinformation of the memory content onto the practice material as a function of the experimental variables:

$$T(G, X) = H(X) - H(X|G). \qquad (3\text{–}14)$$

Since the purpose of memory experiments is to study the mechanisms of information receiving and processing, the unit of measurement for information, and the derived unit of transinformation, are well adapted to the problem.

Informational accommodation to meaningless material can also be measured in this way. In particular, this procedure avoids the systematic error that, when a finite repertory of meaningless syllables or words is used, the subjects come to know its limitations after a certain time. Subjects usually notice when an open repertory is used and, consciously or unconsciously, expect new and different words and syllables of the same class. Hence the subjective information is always larger than the objective information.

In carrying out an experiment, it is necessary to use the usual type of experimental design with parallel groups because measurement of the subjective information is associated with a learning process.

If we take as the unit of measurement for memory experiments subjective information and transinformation, we pick up any semantic and associative aspects which the material may have for the subject, insofar they affect the information. This gives access to a field which is important in empirical research into education. This is the study of memory functions as they relate to meaningful texts and subject matter. These may well include learning processes of a higher order, like classification and category formation.

Memory experiments therefore operate within a continuum ranging from pure storage processes in the case of meaningless materials to complex learning processes as measured in principle in the didactic transinformation.

Let us quote the example of a memory experiment relating to a sophisticated literary text, Erhard Kästner's description of a desert landscape entitled "Die nordafrikanische Wüste". The experiment was carried out in the 7th grade of a Volksschule. All the children read the text slowly and were given 8 minutes in which to study it. The subjective information was then determined for three matched parallel groups ($N = 8$) at different time intervals: 20 minutes, 4 days, and 8 days after reading the text. The information value of the unseen text was determined in a parallel class.

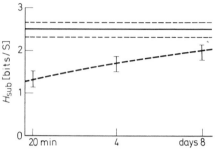

Fig. 3.18   Information as function of time.

Fig. 3.18 shows how the information of the text asymptotically approaches the initial value the longer the time elapsed since receipt of the information; see also note (3/8).

The transinformation (shown in Fig. 3.19) decreases with increasing time since reading. It represents the part of the information received during reading which was still stored in the memory at the time of measurement. This is the memory curve.

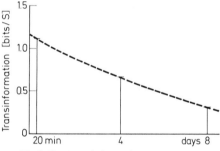

Fig. 3.19   Transinformation, memory curve.

3.7   Cognitive-Process Curve

By measuring and recording the information of every letter in a continuous text we obtain an information profile that indicates which of the signs making up the text contain much or little information. Instead of measuring the average information H_{sub} of longer passages of text, we can use this other way of determining how the information is distributed over the text. There is a decline in information in the middle of a word, and the first few letters have more information than the last. As a word is predicted, the uncertainty as to its continuation decreases in inverse proportion to what is known about the beginning of the word. The method becomes very revealing when, instead of being applied to texts in which the information is fairly evenly distributed, it is applied to the sort of number sequences used in intelligence tests. This gives us a procedure which enables us to observe a model simulating the processes which interest the teacher: the dawning of awareness of a rule in analogy to the formation of categories.

Intelligence tests use number sequences where one number has to be filled in to complete the series of N given numbers; see Amthauer IST. We are interested in the cognitive processes which enable the underlying principle of the number sequence to be recognized. Thus we make the subject predict the sequence term by term from the first term on, and this allows us to measure the information of each term. The principle underlying the sequence is more easily recognized when more terms of the sequence are known. The curve of the information in a successive prediction of such number sequences shows the decline in subjective information as a consequence of insight into the rules determining the sequence.

It is a condition of the test that the subject is not given any prior information about the character of the number sequence. He knows only that it concerns numbers in some particular relationship. He is not told how many terms of the sequence have to be known before the rule can be recognized. Number sequences with stochastic dependences possess a definable information which lies around a constant and approaches a limiting value, whereas the subjective information of a sequence obeying obvious rules may approach zero; see note (3/9). If the subject has achieved an internal model of the rule by heuristic means, the transinformation of this model onto the sequence is equal to the information of the sequence. The subject is then in a position to generate the number sequence and to continue it correctly.

The process of increasing insight into the relationship is indicated by the remaining subjective information as the sequence extends in length.

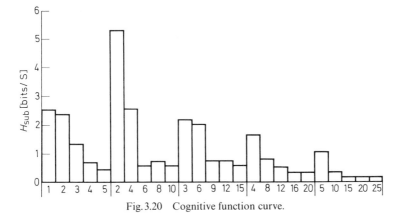

Fig. 3.20   Cognitive function curve.

As in the Jarvik test, which plots the learning process involved in the learning of probability values, this procedure follows the growth of internal models of the rules by recording the decline in subjective information. It is particularly interesting to study series which obey complex rules. A composite rule consisting of several subrules may be regarded as a hierarchy of supersigns. This allows the formation of the various supersigns at different levels to be measured quantitatively. Fig. 3.20 is a sample of the course followed by the subjective information for such a sequence.

The sequence consists of groups of five numbers, each group forming an arithmetic series. The first term in each group moves on by one number. At the beginning of the number sequence, the subjective information falls sharply from the third term onwards, because the subjects are already beginning to expect the continuation of the series of natural numbers. The second group introduces the first change in the rule so that the information rises well above the value for a random sequence. The information peak indicates a high surprise value because the foregoing number sequence had aroused the expectation of a particular continuation so that subjectively other continuations seemed increasingly unlikely.

The information within the second group falls more steeply because the new rule is related to the first one and is recognized more quickly. On passing to the third group, there is on the average another rise in subjective information, but not nearly so pronounced. Thereafter the subjective information falls with each group, and after the fifth group it is virtually zero. It is noteworthy that at the end of the second and third groups the uncertainty, and hence the information, does not decrease because a rule change is now expected even before it occurs.

The cognitive function curve reflects a process. Under ideal conditions, it can be used for the study of cognition relative to defined supersigns and relations. The measurement of the didactic transinformation induced by teaching deals with extremely complex subject matter, and it is difficult to distinguish the proportions due to memorizing, formation of supersigns, and formation of relations. However, for number sequences, it is possible to study the formation of supersigns with and without interference, depending on the experimental design.

Interference may be generated by replacing certain terms in a series by random numbers. Preliminary trials indicated that interference slows the decline in subjective information and that it takes longer to recognize a rule change. This result may also be interpreted as meaning that rules recognized in spite of interference have greater stability. If the stability of the rules so recognized were found to depend upon personality factors, one could assume a certain rigidity.

By adding up the subjective information of each group, we can determine the transinformation of the first group onto the second, the second onto the third, and so on. This often reveals a negative transinformation from the first group onto the second, which is quite understandable since the subject is expecting the rule to continue to operate. On average, the transinformation of one group onto the next is positive. The rule has been recognized when, from a group K onwards, the information of all subsequent groups is zero.

Group Formation as an Aid to Forming Supersigns. When the numbers belonging to a group are visually combined, the subjective information falls more rapidly. This offers a means of investigating empirically the influence which grouping principles exert upon the formation of supersigns. Such groupings are seen by the subject as signals for rule or repertory changes. They are thus aids to supersign formation or to abstraction in the same way as visual aids, and they reduce the subjective information of the transition. The same function is performed by pauses and emphasis when the teacher is addressing the class.

By insight into the rules, we mean the construction of an internal system of relations isomorphic to the rules. The transinformation of this system onto the number sequence is equal to the information of the number sequence itself. This is a learning process. There are two ways of initiating a learning process:

1. A quasi-inductive or heuristic procedure. Here the material to be organized, in this case the number sequence, is presented until the rule is recognized. This was the method used in our experiments, and it enables the influence upon the learning process of the presentation and preparation of the material to be studied separately. The total information of the material which has to be presented before insight into the rules governing the sequence is achieved gives directly the sum of the information which lies below the cognitive function curve.

This procedure is analogous to a lesson in which the objects to be studied are arranged and presented in a particular way and the problem is developed, but the actual work of induction and the associated formation of supersigns is left to the pupil. In mathematics and science, these teaching strategies are known as "exploratory" or "rediscovery" teaching; see Kerschensteiner (1908), Wagenschein (1962) and Weltner (1963). These strategies represent an extreme form of problem-solving.

2. The subject matter is communicated verbally to the subject. In our example, the number sequence might be described as follows:

"The sequence is divided into groups of five numbers. Each group is the beginning of an arithmetic series. The first two terms of the series exhibit the difference characteristic of the series, and the first term in each group moves on by one number. The first number is one."

This description of the series, which uses no mathematical symbols, also contains the information. The reader of the above passage is able to construct an internal model of the series. If he does this, the subjective information of the number sequence will be zero from the start. This is analogous to a lesson where almost everything is presented verbally.

We can now determine the efficiency in terms of information theory of both procedures for our example above. The verbal description of the series is a basic text with respect to the rule, and its didactic information can be measured. This gives the surprising result that the construction of the rule according to the quasi-inductive method requires didactic information of the order of magnitude of only 30 bits, whereas the verbal presentation requires about 90 bits. In this instance the heuristic procedure is superior to verbal explanation from the point of view of efficiency. However, it would be premature to generalize from this finding. Rules of more complex design that involve relations between more distant number groups, or sequences subject to more interference from random numbers could well give rise to a situation where the underlying rules will simply not be recognized. Moreover, it is sometimes observed that subjects give up the search for rules unless they have some definite success within the first 30 numbers. In such cases the information which has to be offered to trigger heuristic processes may reach large values, whereas the information of a verbal presentation remains at about the same order of magnitude as in our example.

Any comparison of the information-theory efficiency of inductive heuristic strategy versus deductive, concept-oriented strategy in supersign formation must be related to the case under consideration. However, it can be done by the methods described above. It would appear that inductive, heuristic procedures are particularly useful in cases where the problem or the subject matter can be isolated, whereas verbalizing methods are more rational for problem-solving that involves overlapping relationships and systematic presentations. Thus it seems that heuristic procedures more readily arouse the problem awareness which motivates the formation of supersigns. In addition to the efficiency in terms of information theory, it is possible to study stability of recall of supersigns formed by heuristic procedures. The effect of drilling, that is, the transfer of successful cognitive processes to heuristic performances with other series, is also worth studying. It may be assumed that transinformation exists with regard to the processes which effect the formation of supersigns.

The cognitive function curve is a tool for examining the process of the rise and fall of the subjective information of sign sequences and, in particular, for observing the formation of supersigns. The interpretation depends on the theoretical models used but is not restricted to information-theory models. As our research has shown, the analysis of the cognitive function curve could be a new and effective method for studying certain problems concerning the psychology of learning and teaching methods.

4 Learning and Teaching in the Light of Information Theory

4.1 The Model of Information Reception and Processing in Man

The description of the psychological phenomena of learning and perception in terms of units of information has enabled us to develop simplified models in which the most important functions of information reception and processing could be expressed quantitatively. Immediately following the development of information theory, many American psychologists made use of the unit of information to study, by means of bivariate information analysis, perception processes, reaction times, and the connection between stimuli and the absolute judgements based on these stimuli; see Quastler (1955); Attneave (1959). Frank (1962) undertook to summarize the detailed results and made the first attempt to construct a model restricted exclusively to the use of concepts that are quantifiable and can be described in terms of information theory. Later, Riedel (1967d) expanded and refined the model. Fig. 4.1 shows a section of the model, simplified but adequate for our purposes.

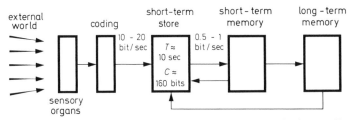

Fig. 4.1 Simplified model of information reception and processing in man (Frank).

Man receives from his environment via the peripheral organs (sensory organs, receptors) and various channels of perception, a great variety of information: optical, acoustic, tactile, also sensations of smell and taste. The information flow impinging upon the sensory organs is enormous: for the optical receptors (eyes) about 10^6 bits per second, for the acoustic receptors (ears) about 10^4 bits per second, but appreciably less for the other receptors. The information perceived is coded and transmitted through neuronal networks and lines. This process reduces the information by several orders of magnitude, for the consciously perceived—or apperceived—information flow is of the order of 10 to 20 bits a second.

In this model, consciousness is described as a short-term store having two characteristics:

1. It takes up information from the environment via the sensory organs, but it has a limited flow rate. At the same time, information can reach the consciousness from the long-term store, memory.

2. Information can be retained wholly in the consciousness for a short period, the present duration. The processing of the information currently held in the consciousness takes place in the present duration, as dicussed in Section 4.2.

Part of the information from the consciousness may be stored in an information store, the memory. This also applies to information derived neither from perception nor memory, but from information processing in the short-term store. Empirical findings force us to assume that there are different kinds of memory, differing in speed of inflow as well as in length of time for which their contents are stored. For a rough distinction, it is sufficient to assume a short-term memory, storing its contents for hours and days, and a long-term memory, storing its contents for months and years. The information stored in the memory can be recalled to the consciousness. In the course of time, the stored information decays or is forgotten. A more complicated model can also take account of information exchanges between the various kinds of memory.

The educationist is interested in the parameters of the various functions and how they change with age.

4.1.1   Inflow Capacity of the Short-Term Store

The size of the perceivable information flow has been determined by a number of different experimental procedures. Studies of reaction time in man to various stimuli (optical—flashing lights; acoustic—Morse signals, etc.) from a predetermined repertory which, however, varied with the various tests, showed that reaction time increased with the information of the stimulus field created by the experimental procedure; see Hick (1952), Hyman (1953).

The reaction time is made up of two components:

a) a constant time interval for transmitting stimuli within the neuronal system;

b) a time that is directly proportional to the information of the stimulus field and that represents the time interval required for the perception system to process the information of the stimuli presented.

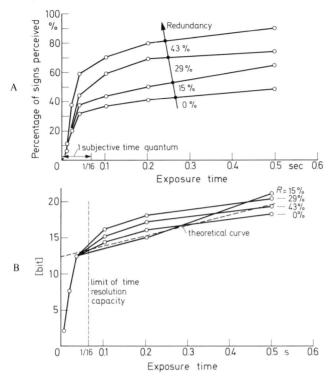

Fig. 4.2   Apperception experiments (Miller, Bruner and Postman). A percentage of signs perceived; B perceived information.

This processing time increases in proportion to the information of the signals; thus, it can be used to determine maximal information flow, which is found to be 16.7 bits a second. Similar experiments where recognition times for letter sequences were determined tachistoscopically are reported by Miller, Bruner and Postman (1954). These authors used meaningless letter combinations which, however, more or less resembled the letter sequences of ordinary written language because they respected the normal digram and trigram combinations. They found that the number of letters perceived per unit of time increased in proportion as the letter sequences used more closely resembled ordinary language. When the information apperceived in this way is worked out, it is found to be independent of the degree of stochastic dependence within the sequence. Given equal exposure time, few signs having high information, or many signs having low information were perceived. The mean information flow rate was 16 bits per second.

Quastler and Wulf, as cited by Attneave (1965), indicate that professional pianists can process 22 bits of information per second, and extempore readers 18 bits per second. In a similar experiment, they determined the information flow rate of meaningless letter sequences copied on the typewriter as 15 bits per second. Hofstätter (1960) estimates the information flow rate in spoken exchanges to be 8 bits per second. In interpreting all such experiments, it is important to remember that the inflow capacity consists of two components, the information of the perceived signs and, if the signs are meaningful (spoken or written language), the semantic information that flows from the memory into the consciousness, in fact, what the signs mean. This is certainly true of spoken exchanges, which give double the information flow rate quoted above.

Riedel (1964) investigated the inflow capacity of the short-term store as a function of age and found that it increases from 9 bits per second at 7 years of age to 18.6 bits per second at 15 years of age. He also evaluated the data in the literature, obtained by various experimental procedures but always with meaningless syntactical material, and compiled a rate-for-age curve (1967); see Fig. 4.3.

The finding common to of all these experiments is that the apperceptible rate of information flow is restricted to a value of between 10 and 20 bits and is virtually the same for both the optical and the acoustic channels of perception.

4.1.2 Present Duration (Gegenwartsdauer)

For a brief, limited period the apperceived information remains in the consciousness. Thus one may count the bell strokes immediately after

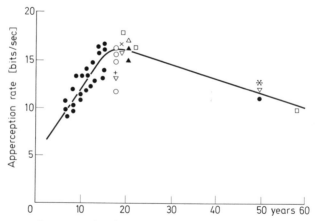

Fig. 4.3   Apperception rate as a function of age (Riedel, 1967c). ● Riedel; △ Brainard 1960; □ Suci et al., 1960; ○ Hyman 1953; △ Griew 1963; + Crossman 1963; × Hall & Ugelow 1957; * Crossman and Szafran 1956; ▲ Raif 1960.

the clock has stopped striking, or repeat word-for-word a sentence just heard or read. This period, also called in psychology psychic present time or duration of immediate retention, is a function of age.

Riedel (1964) determined that the present duration is 3 to 5 seconds at 7 years of age and 8 seconds at 15 years.

Capacity of short-term store: If the flow of apperceived information is about 16 bits per second, and such information can be retained for an average of 6 to 10 seconds, this sets a limit to the capacity of the short-term store. This capacity, which is also age-dependent, has a range of 100 to 160 bits for adults. This fact is described in psychology, though not quantitatively, as "Enge des Bewußtseins" (narrowness of consciousness).

4.1.3   Memory

Riedel has evaluated the speed of inflow into memory in terms of information theory on the basis of the relevant experiments and to the extent permitted by the available data. It is possible to make relatively precise statements concerning the decay of memory with time, since the data are in agreement, but there are very few measurements of inflow capacity available. For the short-term memory, storing information for hours or days, inflow rates of 0.5 to 1.5 bits per second are obtained. For the long-term memory (weeks and years), the values quoted are from 0.05 to 0.2 bit per second. The construction of a more accurate model including several kinds of memory may give a better fit between the model and the experimental observations.

On the basis of our measurements of the didactic transinformation (Section 3.2) we obtain an inflow capacity of 0.2 to 0.5 bit per second. Since these experiments were carried out on average one week after receipt of the information, this gives us the lower limit for the speed of flow into the short-term memory. It may be assumed that, in addition to the didactic information just learned, aesthetic information was also stored. As our measurements specifically excluded aesthetic information, it follows that the total inflow capacity must be greater. The transinformation of once-through reading, which includes both aesthetic and semantic transinformation, was measured in a few experiments and yielded values of 2 to 6 bits per second for the inflow capacity of memory contents which could be recalled 10 to 60 minutes (average 30—40 minutes) after receipt of the information; see note (3/5). Subdivision into more kinds of memory may well be required for a detailed description of memory functions, but for a large number of problems in education the simplified model is adequate. The first point of interest to the educationist in evaluating and interpreting the present findings is the limit to the rate at which information is taken into the short-term store and the memory. This limit must be observed in teaching procedures; it was obtained quantitatively on the basis of psychological investigations, and has been determined by us by applying transinformation analysis to the subjects normally taught in school. It would, however, be of great value for the further development of the model to have more extensive investigations covering such educationally relevant material as subject matter exhibiting different degrees of coherence. No work of this type has yet been done.

4.2   Learning Viewed in the Light of Information Theory

Of the set of all learning processes, we shall look at those covered by the general concept of verbal learning. Though motor learning processes can also be analyzed by means of information theory, we shall consider here only those processes immediately concerned with the perception and processing of information.

The process of learning is the reaction with its environment of a learning system based on information exchange and communication. According to Steinbuch (1960) and Zemanek (1961), the totality of these learning processes is to be understood as the construction of internal models of the external world. Each of these internal models reproduces isomorphically a particular area of a single structure or element in the external environment. This isomorphic reproduction is a boundary value which can be approximated by the internal models constructed by the subject, but need not be attained. One should not read too much into this construction of internal models and suppose that the model represents the entire external world. It is more a matter of constructing fragmentary models and partial structures, each corresponding to a particular domain or element of the external world. The boundary value of such an ideal model occurs when the elements B_j of the model B correspond to the elements A_j of the external domain A. This correspondence must also extend to the relations existing between the individual elements, so that any change in the internal model is isomorphous with respect to a change in the external world, and vice versa.

The internal models therefore represent a reversible and unique picture of the external world. When internal models have been constructed, they will have a transinformation onto the information of the external world. Such models can be deterministic or probabilistic. Since the external environment is in principle a probabilistic system with deterministic components, the internal models may well be fully deterministic, but they will then have less transinformation onto the environment.

In the theory of abstract automata, both the external environment and the learning system may be regarded and represented as an abstract automaton. Itelson (1967) provides a summary and classification of the approaches applying to internal models in the theory of learning (Bush, Mosteller, Estes etc.) from the point of view of the theory of automata. The transinformation of the models onto the external world reaches its maximum when external world and internal model coincide in their degree of determinism; see note (4/1).

Frank (1969) describes learning simply as the reduction of the information of the external world: "A system learns something about its environment by reducing the portion of subjective information about its environment. It can use the information to produce the most appropriate behaviour in this environment, but first it must receive it."

Von Cube (1965) uses the concept of redundancy for his definition of learning which he describes as the reduction of the information of the environment or, expressed positively, the generation of redundancy.

The reduction of the information of the external world by a percipient subject is not possible until he has made an internal model of the environment. For this reason, we give the central place in our study to the various possible ways of constructing internal models and the transinformation of such models onto the environment.

We can use the method of transinformation analysis to measure, along with the transinformation, the efficiency of these models and so determine their degree of isomorphism to the world of objects and to their relationships.

We see learning as the construction of internal models of the external world which in both their present and future structure have a transinformation onto this same environment. There are three sorts of learning processes, already briefly mentioned in Section 3.1:

1. *Storing of information, learning by rote.* A message stored in the memory may now be seen as an internal model of the communication itself. A poem learned by heart is an internal model of the text of the poem as it exists in the form of written signs. What is in the memory is also and at the same time an internal model of the poem recited aloud. The transinformation of the internal model onto the message in either form can reduce its information to zero. What concerns educationists, however, is usually only the storing of the didactic information, not the aesthetic information, whose transinformation reduces only the semantic part of the message.

2. *Learning of probability; informational accommodation.* The information of a field is reduced once the frequency distribution of the various elements is known. If a percipient knows the frequency profile of the field, its information falls. The construction of internal models reproducing the probability and frequency distributions of event fields, on average reduces the information of these fields. The learning process so understood consists in matching subjective expectations to objective

probabilities. Similarly, the code words used by the information-receiving system, and in which the messages in question are physiologically encoded, must be matched to the information of the messages. Knowing the probabilities of occurrence of a field usually gives a faster apperception rate. It is also necessary for the construction of such models that conditional frequencies be taken into account, so that the conditional expectation probabilities, being a function of the boundary conditions of a field, can become the basis for perception. A person may as a result of his internal knowledge adapt to the diction of a particular speaker, and hence anticipate this speaker's expected repertory of words and grammatical patterns. This reduces the information of the sequence of messages transmitted by this speaker. Informational accommodation, or the learning of probability, is thus the construction of internal models of event fields.

3. *Supersign formation by means of*
a) complex formation
b) category formation
c) formation of relationships

Complex formation. Take the complex: "castle". It is made up of a limited number of elements: towers, walls, roofs, windows, loopholes. If an internal model of this combination is constructed, it may be encoded in a word sign. If an internal model corresponds to the word, this word has a transinformation onto all communications in which the word "castle" occurs.

Science and technology make extensive use of supersign formation by means of complex formation. In electronics functional complexes are represented by circuit diagrams:

amplifier unit, microphone, loudspeaker.

Similar complexes are formed in data processing:

peripheral units, input units, output units, accumulator,
memory program.

Complex formation brings about a change in the repertory and generally a reduction in the information, too, when perception occurs in the repertory of supersigns. It is possible to have a switch of repertories so that an object of perception perceived as a supersign can also be perceived in the repertory of the elements. Thus, words can be read letter by letter and electrical circuits can be broken down into their elements. The perceived information increases in such a transition.

Category formation. Various perceived objects may contain certain elements in common. In a given context only the common elements may be relevant and the differences irrelevant. If this is the case, these objects may be combined into one category. Within the category, the irrelevant differences between the objects are ignored.

If, during perception, only the category of an object is perceived and the irrelevant information suppressed, the perceived information of the object belonging to the category is less than the information of the object.

Example a. The same letter can be encoded in a number of ways by different typefaces, but when the sign is read, it is the category of letter that is perceived. Relative to this category, the various typefaces are equivalent objects. However, if the different typefaces were to be perceived as different signs, the use of the four typefaces commonly used in printing would alone increase the information of each letter sign by 2 bits. This information is of the same order of magnitude as the average information of the letter within the text. It is reduced by the transinformation of the internal model of the invariant category of letters onto the sign.

Example b. A school physics laboratory contains a variety of apparatus of different shapes and sizes. Their relevant feature, however, is a certain physical property, namely their "ohmic resistance". The supersign "ohmic resistance" encodes a category and so reduces the information of a laboratory situation or a physical problem field. The formation of the internal model "ohmic resistance" is thus equivalent to encoding by a common sign at the level of signs. Bartlett as early as 1932 described this phenomenon as a process of qualitative simplification of the remembered material.

In category formation, *one* internal model is formed for *any number* of objects in the external world. The model, of course, reproduces only some of the properties of the external objects: those which are common to all. A distinction is made here between relevant and irrelevant information. Thus the internal model has less information than the external object. Perception in the repertory of supersigns formed in this way will lower the information of the external world. A good proportion of teaching processes have as their aim the formation of such supersigns (invariance formation).

Formation of relationships, linking concepts, and internal operators: the presentation of relationships and linking concepts is very important in forming internal models and leads to the construction of internal systems. The formation in these internal systems of deterministic or stochastic dependences between items contained in the consciousness is a reflexive conscious process and has transinformation onto the object domains so reproduced. These object domains may be regarded as product fields. The construction of internal systems differs from supersign formation via the the formation of complexes and categories because here there is no switch of repertory. It is not the elements of perception which are changed by being combined into a product field, but their conditional probabilities. The information of the product field is reduced by the larger transinformation of the internal models onto it. Let us give an example of the transinformation of an internal system onto product fields. Ohm's law is the statement of a relationship between current and potential under certain conditions. If this relationship is internally known, there is trans-information onto the results of any physical experiment, and the information of the experimental data is thereby reduced; see also 2.1.

If we regard learning processes leading to a knowledge of coherence and relationships as the construction of *internal operators,* we can call these operators *second-order supersigns.* The conclusion for education is that it must try to develop such operators by means of learning processes which have a large transinformation onto the external world in as many and as relevant situations as possible; see note (4/2).

4.2.1   Transinformation, Redundancy, "Informedness"

It is mathematically equivalent to describe learning processes as the reduction of the subjective information of the external world (Frank), the generation of redundancy (von Cube), or the construction of internal models with transinformation onto the external world. Itelson (1967) introduces the concept of "informedness" (Informiertheit) (K) to describe the internal state. K is the measure of the reduction in the uncertainty of a situation H_0 due to knowledge H_1:

so that
$$H_1 = H_0 - K \qquad\qquad (4\text{--}1)$$
$$K = H_0 - H_1. \qquad\qquad (4\text{--}2)$$

Thus K is identical with the transinformation T of knowledge onto the situation. See note (4/3).

We are proposing that the concept of *transinformation* be used as the fundamental concept of information theory in dealing with educational questions. This is because internal models or states cannot be observed and analyzed directly but only indirectly through their effects. We measure these effects as transinformation onto product fields. This gives us observable values on which to base our argument. It does not, however, provide a description of the internal models, since we wish to avoid any unnecessary restriction on the formation of future concepts such as could arise from equating the models with a value derived from them.

4.3   Elements of a Theory of Teaching

The model of information reception and processing in man and the empirical findings presented in Chapter 3 furnish some important pointers towards an elementary theory of teaching. A necessary but not always sufficient precondition for any kind of teaching is that the limits which govern the reception and processing of information be observed.

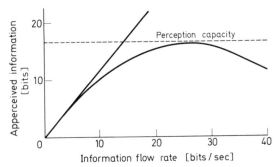

Fig. 4.4   Apperceived information as a function of information flow.

4.3.1   Limits of Perception Capacity

In the adult, the inflow rate to the short-term store averages 16 bits per second. So long as the flow of information from the teaching system does not exceed this limit and the message does not include any signs unknown to the recipient, it can be assumed that he will perceive all or nearly all of the information. If the information flow increases beyond the apperception rate, the perceived information will fall. In teaching, the flow of information is mainly in speech form. When the flow exceeds the apperception rate, the result must be that the recipient no longer receives all the signs correctly and so fails to grasp the context which reduces the information of the individual signs. When coherent perception ceases. the subjective information of the individual signs increases yet again and the proportion of correctly perceived information falls still further.

Fig. 4.4 gives a curve which shows how apperceived information depends on the rate at which information is offered.

What the teacher says. The teacher uses a more comprehensive repertory of words and grammatical forms than the pupil does. His task is moreover to present new subject matter, so that he is forced to use a sign repertory subjectively rich in information for the pupil. Thus, it can easily happen that the information flow conveyed by what the teacher says exceeds the pupil's inflow capacity. The boundary conditions to be satisfied by what the teacher says are easier to formulate than to observe.

The speed at which he talks must be adapted to the age-dependent perception capacity of the pupils; the average sentence length—to be more precise, the sentence duration—must be adapted to their age-dependent present duration; and the sign repertory must agree with that of the pupils.

The last requirement is in principle not fully attainable, since building up and expanding the sign repertory is the special task of teaching. The teacher is required to construct new signs, introduce new concepts and explain new relationships in such a way that he uses known words, concepts and relationships and explains unknown signs by means of known ones.

Visual media. Pictures, slides, sectional models and, in science teaching, experimental set-ups and similar arrangements, have an information value which is completely perceived only after careful study. More information is presented than can be taken in at one time. Conversely, the build-up of a drawing on the backboard limits the information flow because only as much new information is added per unit of time as can be apperceived. This makes it easier to concentrate attention on the new elements being introduced because they stand out better from their environment and are richer in information. The inherent advantage of using blackboard drawings can also be utilized in slides by breaking down information-rich illustrations into slide sequences. In order that the *newly* introduced elements stand out very clearly, the existing material must be made information-poor by remaining unaltered. The same elementary information-theory approach can be used for experimental set-ups in science teaching. The apparatus is not presented in fully assembled form but set up during the lesson so as to enable the information of the experimental arrangement to be taken in currently as the lesson proceeds.

4.3.2   Limits of Memory Inflow Capacity

We cannot speak of learning until the didactic information has been retained as well as perceived. A comparison of speed of inflow into the memory and speed of apperception shows that only 5% of the apperceived information is stored in the memory. This value is exceeded only by memories with a "half-life" of minutes to hours.

The information perceived during teaching comprises a didactic (semantic) part and an aesthetic part. If the didactic information — and this can include supersigns newly constructed by information processing in the short-term memory — is to be stored in the memory proper, the speed of inflow of the didactic information must not exceed the inflow capacity of the memory. The dilemma inherent in any type of information transmission, whether by teaching or learning, is that the inflow capacity of the memory is smaller than perception capacity by more than an order of magnitude. As a rule, lectures and instructional programs on radio or TV are designed to allow their information flow to be perceived by the recipient, but they are not necessarily adapted to the far more stringent limitation of memory inflow capacity. Teaching, however, must ensure that the didactic information is retained and that the internal models constructed will, even after a certain time lapse, still have some transinformation onto the external world.

During teaching, the didactic information flow must be reduced for the recipient by repetitions, questions and exchanges, all on the same topic. However, this does not fully occupy the perception capacity, so that the pupil is in danger of switching his attention to other sources of information; therefore, it is necessary to maintain an aesthetic information flow. By presenting the same subject matter in a variety of ways, by changing the repertory in which it is offered, and with the use of drawings and visual media, the same didactic information may be held in the short-term store for a fairly long time so as to enable it to be transferred to the memory.

Varying the aesthetic information also encourages the formation of invariants and improves discrimination between relevant and irrelevant information. Here the teacher needs to be aware of the particular difficulty that, for him, the didactic information of the teaching material is zero, so he will tend to underestimate the rate of didactic information flow for the pupils. During his training he must develop the ability to generate aesthetic information around a given subject to be taught. In other words, he must be able to express a given subject matter in a wide range of presentations, to look at it from several points of view and to break it down into as many separate problems as possible.

Learning in context. The conditional information, or the information in context, is on average always less than the information of isolated elements. It follows that the elements of a given subject have less information when in context. Once relationships between perceived elements have been recognized, the internal model of interdependent elements has less information than that of independent ones. Subject matter presented in context therefore has an increased probability of being stored and retained in the pre-alerted memory.

Textbooks. The didactic information in textbook-type presentations is so large that once-through reading will far exceed memory inflow capacity. This is particularly true of texts which employ a word repertory that deviates from everyday language. Textbooks are frequently coherent texts with definite relationships between the various parts of the text, so that an additional difficulty for the reader is that in a normal reading of the text the information is perceived but not retained. In consequence, it is difficult to recognize relationships between parts of the text which lie far apart in the book.

Programmed instruction. Teaching programs must have a didactic information flow which matches inflow capacity, just as the teacher must. This applies both to teaching programs in book form and to programmed instruction by teaching machines. Teaching programs have the external form of a cycle of short statements and questions which together make up one frame. These questions have a dual function.

The question is designed to check whether the program user has correctly perceived the didactic information contained in the frame. A wrong answer indicates insufficient didactic transinformation, and an adaptive teaching machine can introduce an additional frame or series of frames until the desired didactic transinformation is achieved.

Since the question as a rule contains no new didactic information, it will be held invariant in the consciousness while the answer is being given. This reduces the didactic information flow by a factor of two to three.

Skill in developing teaching programs thus demands that aesthetic information be generated by varying formulations and by changing the repertory of presentation. Although the didactic information flow has to be reduced to match inflow capacity, the program must not bore the user. The expert may find the numerous repetitions frustrating, but this is how optimization of the didactic information flow is achieved. From the amount of didactic information in the teaching material, as determined by transinformation analysis of the basic text, we can estimate the required teaching time by assuming that the inflow capacity of the memory for didactic information is 0.5 bit per second. The age dependence of inflow capacity is also taken into account for school subjects.

The didactic information flow in teaching programs can be monitored by means of the $m-i$ diagram introduced by Anschütz (1965). Each new concept introduced is entered in a diagram covering a sequence of frames. This yields an average advance in concepts per *frame*. If the didactic information of the concepts is also known, then the didactic information flow can be calculated. For practical purposes, one may use an average figure for didactic information per concept when checking the development of the program with the diagram.

Checking the didactic information flow is also the object of the $w-t$ system; Frank (1966). In this approach, the average advance in concepts per *unit of time* is determined while the teaching program is being worked out. In developing programs according to the $w-t$ system, the advance in concepts is compared with norms established for certain classes of users and subject matter. A concept in this system is any word in the basic text above a certain point in Meier's (1964) word rank list.

4.3.3   Limits of Capacity of Short-Term Store

The limits of the capacity of the short-term store—80–160 bits according to age—restrict the formation of supersigns. Supersigns can be formed by means of reflexive conscious processes only from elements simultaneously present in the short-term store.

This places a double constraint on the formation of the less information-rich supersigns. Elements between which a relationship has been recognized, or from which a new concept will be formed, must reach the short-term store within the limited present duration and within the limits of the speed of perception. Supersign formation is facilitated when the elements are presented or arranged so as to meet this condition. During our research on the cognitive process function, it was found that the speed with which rules are recognized is inversely proportional to the distance separating the signs which obey the rule.

Supersign formation is also inhibited if, when switching to a topic new to the the student, informational accommodation is not accomplished. Because of the large subjective information of the new field of perception, fewer elements can be simultaneously present in the short-term store. Informational accommodation depends on intelligence; weaker pupils are at a disadvantage if there is a change of subject each hour, because they find it particularly difficult to perform the required adaptation; see Frank (1962). The disadvantage for the weak pupil is not so much that he cannot perceive the didactic information as that, until he has made the accommodation, the individual elements have more subjective information so that fewer elements are held present and supersign formation is thereby restricted.

The recognition of relationships is encouraged indirectly by looking at the problem or the topic for some time from several aspects and surveying the scope of the question or problem from as many angles as possible. The frequent occurrence of the same or similar concepts will reduce the information of the problem field. Informational accommodation reduces the subjective information for the pupil, so that he can hold several elements present at the same time. This increases the probability that he will recognize the relationships between them and form internal models.

The converse of this effect is seen when unfamiliar signs are substituted for frequently used signs, as the former have more information.

Example. In a physics lesson, the pressure of a fluid is given as a function of immersion depth *s* by the formula

$$p(s) = p_0 + \rho \cdot s.$$

The pupil often has difficulty in grasping the simple mathematical relationships expressed by this formula. If the same relation is written in the form he has been taught in mathematics:

$$y = ax + b,$$

he readily understands the relationship.

Since unfamiliar signs have more subjective information, the unfamiliar way of writing all the symbols in the first formula may have so much subjective information that the relationship expressed by the equation exceeds the capacity of the short-term store and is not intellectually comprehended. If such a case occurs during teaching, the subjective information of the relation may be reduced by transposing it to the familiar formulation.

When a relationship is to be recognized, it is helpful to give examples consisting of elements having small subjective information. This is indeed the value of examples. They make it easier for the student to recognize the formal structure of a second-order supersign (relation) such as he is required to form, because the small information of the elements in the examples enables him to keep the whole complex present in his mind.

Programmed teaching. Programmed teaching is designed to ensure that intended supersign formation, which may well be essential for further progress in learning, will occur with high probability. In measuring out the frames, we match them to the limited capacity of the short-term store without reference to our information-theory justification. There are three successive phases in working through a frame:

receive information

perceive the question

answer and check whether right or wrong.

In designing a frame, we assume each stage has a present duration of 10 seconds, which gives an optimal working time of 30 seconds per teaching element. This time is probably too short, because answering a question often requires more time than present duration. While the question is being answered, the contents of consciousness may remain in the short-

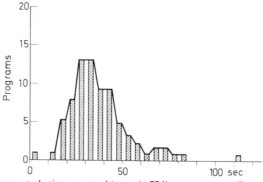

Fig. 4.5   Average study time per teaching unit, 77 linear programs (Programs 63).

term store for longer than one present duration if fed in again by reflexive conscious processes (perseveration).

Fig. 4.5 shows a compilation of the average time taken to work through a frame in those American teaching programs for which empirical data are available; source: Programs 63.

The bunching of the average working time around the value 30 to 40 seconds can be seen as independent confirmation of the utility of the model concept of information theory, as well as a handy rule for writing teaching programs. Direct measurements of the subjective information of frames were made on random samples from three programs; the values obtained were between 80 and 200 bits; see Weltner (1966). Thus the average information per word in teaching programs is only half that found in normal texts. This provides empirical proof of informational accommodation to the altered frequency distribution of word fields found within the teaching program. This finding ought also to apply to spoken communication during teaching. As a result, the number of concepts held present is increased so that they are available for supersign formation.

Organization, Supersign Hierarchy. Since the limited capacity of the short-term store precludes the direct formation of internal models, it is necessary when teaching complex subjects to build up a hierarchy of models or supersigns.

Suppose the pupil cannot grasp right away how a refrigerator works and how the coolant is circulated; it is first necessary to present auxiliary concepts and their relationships, such as why evaporation lowers the temperature, and the function of evaporator, compressor, condenser, and capillaries. This gives rise to partial models or auxiliary supersigns. Finally, this restricted repertory of related partial models gives an insight into the overall relationship.

Thus a supersign hierarchy is created, insight into the overall relationship being effected from the repertory of partial models formed into complexes, while detailed information can always be made available by switching repertories.

Von Cube (1962) used empirical memory experiments with numerical sequences to show that memory performance increases with organization of the sequence; he put forward a mathematical model to explain this finding. Lansky (1967) generalized this mathematical theorem and solved the problem of the reduction of the subjective information of a field by means of organization and supersign formation. This, however, requires the assumption that internal supersign formation within the supersign hierarchy is completed by means of learning processes. Since only a limited number of signs can be held present at each supersign level, any insight into highly structured relationships presupposes the formation of supersign hierarchies over several steps; see also Miller (1954).

During teaching, the construction of supersign hierarchies may be facilitated by their organization and combination under concepts of higher order. In addition, an explanation of the organization and derivation of the themes being taught will reinforce the process of informational accommodation in the pupil. Such an explanation will enable him to consciously adjust to the changing frequency distributions within the repertories assigned to particular themes, so that he need not relearn each repertory every time via the actual frequency distribution.

Helping learning processes by limiting the repertory. In learning situations, the subjective information of the field often exceeds the capacity of the short-term store. It is possible to adjust to this limited capacity by reducing the field, but the structure of the learning situation must not be destroyed in so doing.

Example. The difficulty for the novice chess player is that the information of the possible moves of the chessmen and the game situations exceed the capacity of the short-term store. His dilemma is that, on the one hand, he cannot master the game strategies until the information of the possible moves has been sufficiently reduced by informational accommodation; on the other hand, he can achieve this only by playing frequently. So long as he does not know the strategies, he will find the game frustrating.

A reduction in game information can be achieved by reducing the repertory (game inventory). With a reduced repertory, game strategies can be used right from the start.

Learning Phase 1. Only the pawns are used. Their moves are learned, and strategy development is encouraged by playing with an intermediate goal. The winner is the one who gets a pawn to the last row of his opponent's squares. Playing this kind of game, the novice is learning the strategies of playing with pawns. When informational accommodation has occurred, he can proceed to:

Learning Phase 2. Pawns and castles are used. Intermediate goal: the winner captures all his opponent's pieces.

In the same manner, the figure repertory is expanded via eight learning phases as soon as informational accommodation to the previous repertory is complete.

Games with limited repertories represent a model for teaching how to build up complex modes of behavior within the limited capacity of the short-term store.

4.3.4 Readability Diagrams

Readability is not a sharply defined concept. It is the interaction between a reader and a given text and is characterized by two parameters: the text, and the internal state of the reader. Fucks (1968) has obtained text-related criteria for readability from studies of linguistic statistics.

A unit of readability, designed to measure readability for a given group of readers, must use at the very least one unit of measurement which is objective and text-related, and one which is subjective and related to the reader's internal state.

Objective characteristics:

sentence length; average number of words or syllables per sentence; word length; average number of signs or syllables per word;

statistics, i.e. data on the frequency of certain sentence structures, certain classes of words, etc.

Subjective characteristics:

subjective information of the text; reader's word repertory; reader's subject knowledge.

A simple measure of readability must include at least one objective and one subjective value, for instance:

average sentence length

subjective information.

Both values can be entered on a graph for various text samples; see Fig. 4.6, Weltner (1968). The diagram shows the values for texts and experimental groups obtained from the experiments discussed in Chapter 3.

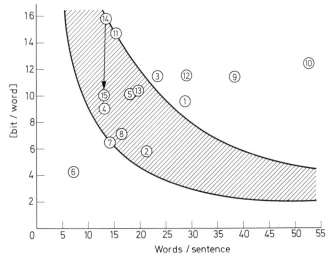

Fig. 4.6   Readability diagram. 1 DIE ZEIT, leading article; 2 DIE ZEIT, biography; 3 DER SPIEGEL, Über die Sprache der Delphine; 4 Textbook about dolphins; 5 Physics textbook, Pohl; 6 Teaching program, 4-stroke engine; 7 Teaching program, Heat; 8 Novel, Mein Vaterhaus; 9 Derbolav, Didaktik I; 10 Derbolav, Didatik II; 11 Business news; 12 Technical text, SPIEGEL, sea water desalination; 13 Technical text, UMSCHAU, sea water desalination; 14 Basic text, 4-stroke engine, 6th grade, before programmed instruction; 15 Basic text, 4-stroke engine, 6th grade, after programmed instruction.

Sentences are logical units and logical relations exist between their elements. A sentence cannot be understood until all its elements are present in the short-term store. If a text is to be understood after once-through reading, it must be possible to be simultaneously conscious of the beginning and the end of a sentence or train of thought. This means that the information of a sentence should be of the order of magnitude of 80–200 bits. This gives a readability zone (hatched in the diagram in Fig. 4.6).

Texts which fall below this zone are trivial, and those above it cannot be properly understood by once-through reading. This is borne out by the known fact that such texts become intelligible after repeated reading, interpretation, and analysis. The zone is bounded on the upper left by values for words which contain as much subjective information as scrambled texts. Here the transinformation from the grammatical and logical coherence onto the word sequences approaches zero; in other words, the reader is quite unaware of the factual and grammatical coherence of the passage.

The modern trend of written language has long been towards shorter sentences. This reflects a preference for texts meant to be comprehensible on once-through reading; it is no longer assumed that readers have time for thorough study.

The condition derived above for the sentence applies equally to the language of the teacher, the lecturer, and the public speaker, as well as to the writing of programmed teaching texts.

Our definition of the readability zone neglects the additional constraints discovered in Miller's investigations (1954). Miller found that the short-term store is limited not only with respect to information, but also in regard to the number of elements simultaneously held present. Miller indicates that about 7 ± 2 elements can be simultaneously present in the consciousness.

4.4   Elements of a Theory Relating to Basic Texts

4.4.1   Coherence Structure Diagram

Any subject matter available in the form of a basic text may be split up into basic text elements. We understand a basic text element to be a self-contained, logical statement that may consist of a combination of two or more concepts, and the definition or explanation of a relationship between concepts. The individual elements may be either interdependent or independent. One basic text element is dependent upon another when it cannot be understood without knowledge of the other element. Independent elements can each be understood separately without reference to the other elements. The following rule applies both to the basic text and to the teaching algorithms derived from it: the sequence in which the basic text elements are presented is restricted by the relationships which exist between them. Interdependent basic text elements must be presented in the right order, i.e. the dependent element must not occur before the element on which it depends.

Before the basic text is written, it is thus necessary to analyze the relationships between the elements on the basis of the subject matter. The block-diagram technique is useful for this purpose. Each block is a box containing an abstract of the contents of a basic text element. When one basic text element presupposes knowledge of another, they are joined by an arrow. By this technique we obtain network plans which indicate the coherence of a subject to be taught. We call them *teaching network plans* or *coherence structure diagrams*. We can distinguish two extreme cases.

Noncoherent Subject Matter. Let us take as an example the subject "Italy" for which we have four basic text elements:

1	The capital of Italy is Rome. Rome lies on the Tiber.

2	Italy is a parliamentary democracy The monarchy was abolished by a plebiscite after the second world war.

3	Industry is concentrated in Northern Italy. Industrialization has recently been encouraged in Southern Italy.

4	Italy is a peninsula; it is shaped like a boot and is surrounded by the Mediterranean Sea.

Each of these four basic text elements can be understood in isolation and none presupposes knowledge of another; they are thus independent of one another. The coherence structure diagram consists of four boxes or "points" not connected with other boxes.

Coherent Subject Matter. Here we take as our example voltage amplification by means of a triode, in a much simplified presentation; see also Fig. 4.7.

| 1 | An alternating voltage U_g applied to the grid regulates the current I_A flowing through the tube. |

| 2 | The anode current I_A flowing through the load resistor R produces at R_A an alternating potential U_{RA} which is larger than U_g. |

| 3 | The anode must have a positive potential. Therefore at point A there is an alternating potential U_{RA}, and a positive direct potential U_A. |

| 4 | An *RC* circuit separates the alternating current from the direct current at point A and transfers it to the grid of the next tube. |

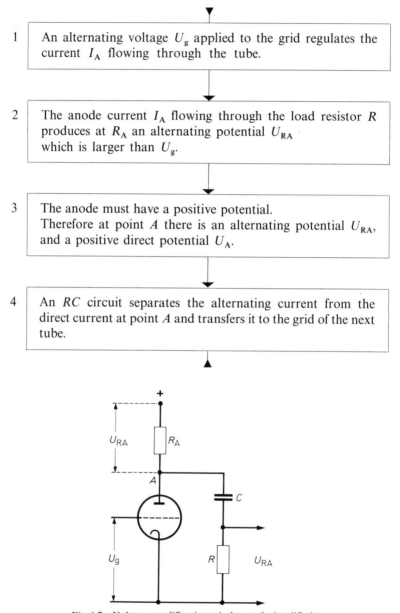

Fig.4.7   Voltage amplification triode, much simplified.

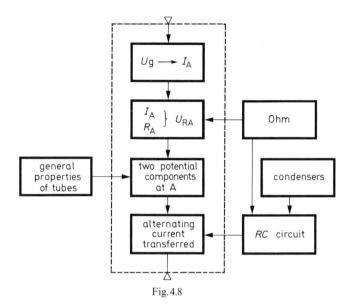

Fig. 4.8

Here the basic text elements are no longer independent, each presupposing knowledge of the preceding one. Further, the second element presupposes a knowledge of Ohm's law, that is, the relationship between current and potential in a resistor. The third element assumes a knowledge of the general properties of tubes, and the fourth a knowledge of the function and operation of RC circuits. This requires a knowledge of Ohm's law and the properties of condensers. The complete coherence structure diagram is shown in Fig. 4.8.

Within the basic text the elements must have a linear arrangement, so the network must be converted into a sequence. In the example given above, it is quite clear how this should be done, but this is not necessarily the case with complicated coherence structure diagrams, although the number of possible arrangements is always finite.

In the above example we have assumed that certain defined relations not explained in the basic text are known. The part of the diagram enclosed by a dotted line in Fig. 4.8 represents the actual subject matter. These basic text elements make up a complete basic text, provided the student already has the knowledge presupposed for elements 2, 3 and 4. If he has not, the basic text is incomplete and must be supplemented by an auxiliary basic text. The iteration method for the empirical investigation of incomplete basic texts is described in Section 3.3.

The construction of coherence structure diagrams is an aid to the logical analysis of the subject to be taught and hence to the development of teaching algorithms. To develop a linear teaching program, all that is required is that the coherence structure diagram be converted into a sequence of basic text elements with due regard to their interdependence. The development of a teaching algorithm for an adaptive teaching system (teacher or adaptive machine) first yields the intersections with the knowledge the student is assumed to have. These are the points where it must be possible to insert teaching sequences in the form of additional loops that can be worked if the assumed knowledge is lacking.

Each basic text element has its own sequence of teaching frames or procedures by means of which the knowledge of the subject matter expressed in the basic text is built up. At the end of the sequence there are check questions designed to reveal whether the required value of didactic transinformation has been reached and, if not, which basic text element assumed too much knowledge. The extra loop can then be used to correct this omission.

If the didactic information of each basic text element is determined by means of transinformation analysis, it is possible to estimate the teaching time required and use this as a basis for writing a program according to "$w - t$ didactics"[4] or some other programming technique.

The method of the coherence structure diagram may be adapted to larger units. We then speak, not of basic text elements, but of teaching blocks which are in fact elements of the curriculum; see Frank (1969).

Lansky in his logical analysis of subjects (1969) carried out a breakdown of basic text elements into basic text words. In this way he obtained an optimal distribution of basic text words; see also 3.3. Lansky formalized his theorem to the extent that he determined the concepts required to explain each new basic text word and then worked out on a computer solely by means of algorithms the optimum order of the basic text words on the basis of their logical relationships to one another.

4.4.2   Teaching Success as a Function of Coherence of Subject Matter

In teaching coherent subjects, success in teaching the whole subject matter depends much more on success with the individual basic text elements than it does in teaching non-coherent subjects. Let p_j be the probability that the didactic information I_{Dj} of the basic text element j has been learned. This probability depends on the amount of time devoted to the basic text element within the teaching period and on the di-

---

[4] $w - t$-Didaktik (word-time didactics) is a method for checking the number of new concepts introduced into audio-visual programs per unit of time. This term is usual in the German literature.

dactic information of that element. It will now be shown that for equal values of p_j, that is, for equal time devoted to teaching each element, the teaching success, that is, the didactic transinformation, is less for coherent subject matter than it is for non-coherent.

For a non-coherent basic text the didactic transinformation is equal to the sum of the didactic transinformation of all basic text elements. The didactic transinformation for the element j is

$$I_{Dj} \cdot p_j,$$

that is, it is equal to the product of the didactic information and the probability that this has been learned.

The total didactic transinformation is then given by

$$T = \sum_{j=1}^{r} I_{Dj} p_j. \tag{4-3}$$

The relative teaching success is then given by the didactic transinformation divided by the didactic information,

$$L = \frac{\sum_{i=1}^{r} I_{Dj} p_j}{I_D}. \tag{4-4}$$

For the special case where all p_j's are equal, the formula reduces to

$$L = p_j = \text{const.}$$

Thus, in a numerical example where all p_j's are equal and their value is 0.8, the relative teaching success is 80%.

Coherent Subject Matter. We begin by simplifying and assume that knowledge supposed known and hence not given in basic text elements is known with probability 1. The probability that the didactic information of a basic text element will be learned then depends on two parameters:

1) the probability p_j that the didactic information will be learned as a result of the teaching sequence;

2) the number of students who conform to the assumption made when the teaching sequence was prepared, i.e. those who have learned the didactic information of the preceding basic text elements.

Taking an ideal case, we consider that didactic transinformation occurs only when the assumption is fulfilled and, if it is not fulfilled, the teaching success is zero. The model can then be worked out. The didactic transinformation of a basic text element j is then equal to the didactic information of the basic text element multiplied by the product of all p_k, thus extending the running variable k to all basic text elements assumed to be known:

$$T_j = I_{Dj} \cdot \prod p_k. \tag{4-5}$$

Then the total didactic transinformation will be

$$T = \sum_{j=1}^{r} I_{Dj} \cdot \prod_{k=1}^{j} p_k. \qquad (4\text{--}6)$$

The product of the probabilities is thus extended to all probabilities relating to the basic text elements assumed to be known. We can formalize the theorem already expressed in the formula by arranging the basic text elements in the sequence of the basic text. Then for all p_k's of basic text elements on which element j does not depend we can insert the value 1. It can easily be shown that for equal didactic information of the basic text elements, the didactic transinformation of coherent teaching materials is smaller than that of incoherent ones. The relative teaching success is given by

$$L = \frac{\sum_{j=1}^{r} I_{Dj} \prod_{k=1}^{j} p_k}{I_{D}}. \qquad (4\text{--}7)$$

In our numerical example, where we now make the further simplifying assumption that all I_{Dj}'s are equal and all p_j's are constant and equal to 0.8, we obtain a relative teaching success of 60%.

If we consider that teaching success is not achieved until the overall context has been understood, i.e. the last basic text element r has also been learned, we have

$$\bar{L}_r = \prod_{k=1}^{r} p_k \qquad (4\text{--}8)$$

in our numerical example:

$$\bar{L}_4 = 0.8 \cdot 0.8 \cdot 0.8 \cdot 0.8 = 0.41.$$

Our conclusion may now be applied to any number of coherence structure diagrams. If the diagram falls into several independent networks, these must considered separately. The procedure can be further formalized by the use of a matrix. For interdependent basic text elements, the prob-

Example :

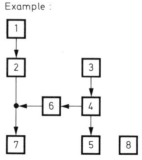

Fig. 4.9   Coherence structure diagram.

abilities of their didactic transinformation are inserted in the cells of the matrix; for independent elements, the value 1 is entered. Dependent elements are those which are linked via any number of intermediate steps within the coherence structure diagram. The products appearing in formulas (4–6) and (4–7) are then the products of all entries in one cell.

Matrix for the calculation of the didactic transinformation when the p'_j s are as shown in the example above

j $\diagdown$ ^{k}	1	2	3	4	5	6	7	8	$I_{Dj} \prod p_k:$
1	p_1	1	1	1	1	1	1	1	$I_{D1} \cdot p_1$
2	p_1	p_2	1	1	1	1	1	1	$I_{D2} \cdot p_1 \cdot p_2$
3	1	1	p_3	1	1	1	1	1	$I_{D3} \cdot p_3$
4	1	1	p_3	p_4	1	1	1	1	$I_{D4} \cdot p_3 \cdot p_4$
5	1	1	p_3	p_4	p_5	1	1	1	$I_{D5} \cdot p_3 \cdot p_4 \cdot p_5$
6	1	1	p_3	p_4	1	p_6	1	1	$I_{D6} \cdot p_3 \cdot p_4 \cdot p_6$
7	p_1	p_2	p_3	p_4	1	p_6	p_7	1	$I_{D7} \cdot p_1 \cdot p_2 \cdot p_3 \cdot p_4 \cdot p_6 \cdot p_7$
8	1	1	1	1	1	1	1	p_8	$I_{D8} \cdot p_8$

It is apparent from the above that for equal time allowed for teaching or programming and for equal didactic information, relative teaching success will be less for coherent subjects than for non-coherent ones. This emphasizes the fact that missing knowledge blocks further learning. If, when constructing teaching algorithms or planning instruction, we insert values for complete teaching success in each individual section of the program, it is immediately apparent that we have to work with higher values for coherent subject matter. This is particularly true of mathematical and scientific subject matter, because it has a high degree of coherence. It follows from what we have said that repetition and drilling are essential in these subjects. The coherence of this type of subject matter may be one of the reasons why teaching success is frequently disappointingly poor here. The construction of a supersign hierarchy is always necessary in coherent subject matter. The analysis of the structure of the subject matter by means of coherence structure diagrams together with

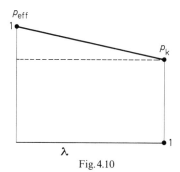

Fig. 4.10

the empirical procedure for determining the complete didactic information by the iteration procedure thus allows the extent of any teaching assignment to be quantitatively estimated.

Note. The model may be refined by using various levels for the strength of the relationship between basic text elements. Let λ be a coherence factor which is zero for independence and unity for maximum dependence. Then an effective probability can be entered in the matrix, expressed as follows:

$$p_{jk\,\text{eff}} = 1 - \lambda_{jk}(1 - p_k). \tag{4-9}$$

4.5   Insight and Transfer

4.5.1   Insight

Insight into the solution of a problem, an exercise, or a relationship, means that an isomorphous internal model of the problem field has been formed. The transinformation of this model reduces the information of the problem field to zero. When an internal model is formed, there is simultaneously discrimination between the relevant and irrelevant information of the problem field. The model is formed from the relevant elements and relationships, therefore its information is less than that of the larger problem field. The elements of the model are not independent of one another, which further reduces their information.

Internal model formation is a reflexive conscious process which takes place in the short-term store prior to transfer into memory. The reduction of information during internal model formation increases the probability that relationships into which insight has been achieved will be retained, relative to the probability for elements of a noncoherent field.

Cognitive processes leading to insight are often combined with an evidential or "aha" experience. The evidential experience is preceded by a phase during which virtual models of the problem field are formed; these, however, fail to trigger the evidential experience so long as their transinformation onto the problem field remains small or, to put it another way, so long as the virtual models are not isomorphous reproductions of the problem field. The problem field may be restructured internally in any number of ways by the formation of virtual models.

The elementary model of information reception in man (see 4.1) owes a great deal to the works of Ebbinghaus and memory psychology; our discussion now moves towards the problems of Gestalt psychology and thought psychology.

When the problem field is restricted, we can use the cognitive process function (see 3.7) to identify the cognitive processes which lead to insight into a system of rules. However, the course of the subjective information will only reveal the transinformation of the virtual models onto the sign sequence and, as transinformation increases, the formation of isomorphous models. To explain the structure of the virtual models generated as solution starters, introspection methods are needed.

Jokes have a cognitive structure similar to that of an evidential experience. The analysis of the cognitive aspect of a joke is of considerable interest because the process can also be examined in a restricted field and can stand as a model case for cognition.

A joke comprises a plot, the development of a situation, a conversation or a happening, all constructed in due sequence. The dénouement has to fulfill two conditions:

1. It has to stand in due sequence in the context of the logical and associative development of the plot. But it does not represent the expected continuation and thus has more subjective information and a certain surprise value. It is not the surprise value alone, however, which triggers the joke experience. For this, a further condition has to be fulfilled.

2. The dénouement must be part of a second, semantic or syntactic context which is independent of the first and is suddenly revealed to the hearer.

The dénouement is thus the element which is common to two independent, logically semantic sequences. Consequently, it has only few degrees of freedom in its formulation and its aesthetic information is slight, sometimes approaching zero. The joke experience occurs when the second context becomes evident, and the initially high subjective information of the dénouement suddenly collapses.

Jokes and insight are congruent with respect to evidential experience. The difference consists in the preceding phase. In the problem-solving situation, virtual models are actively formed and relationships are sought within the problem field. With the joke, the evidential experience comes as a surprise.

If this analysis of the joke is correct, it should be demonstrable by transinformation analysis. The subjective information of the joke must then have the value of normal texts with a steep rise at the dénouement. After the evidential experience, the dénouement should have very slight information or none at all. This can be verified by determining the subjective information of the joke again at a later time. The text in which the joke is being built up should retain some subjective information whereas that of the dénouement should fall sharply.

This situation was in fact shown to exist in empirical experiments with a series of jokes. Fig. 4.11 shows the typical course of the subjective information.

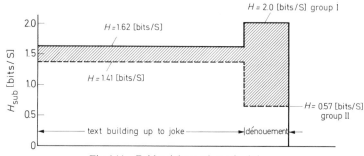

Fig. 4.11   Evidential experience for jokes.

The average values for the text and dénoument of the joke are shown. The dénouement occurs at the end. The higher value applies to group I who have not previously heard the joke, and the lower one to group II who have heard it. For group I, the dénouement has a higher subjective information than the text of the joke, while for group II, it is significantly lower. The difference between the two curves yields the transinformation of knowing the joke onto the joke text. In the area of the dénouement, the transinformation is extremely large because of the occurrence of the evidential experience.

One may also interpret this result as indicating that, once insight has been achieved, the relationship is remembered more easily.

Cognitive processes during learning can be influenced by teaching techniques; see 4.3. Matching the didactic information flow to the user's perception and processing speed is a necessary but not a sufficient condition. The didactic information flow must in addition consist of information which can contribute to the solution of the problem.

A distinction has to be made between relevant and irrelevant didactic information. Irrelevant didactic information either relates to subject matter which the recipient already knows, or it is information which does not contribute solving the problem. Irrelevance also arises when the recipient has already formed supersigns of higher order, yet the didactic information flow is still occurring in the repertory of elementary subsigns. The didactic information has to be adjusted to the awareness of the problem and the level of insight achieved. If this is not done, cognitive processes can be inhibited in two ways:

1. The flow of didactic information is too small because it contains too much irrelevant information. The relevant elements are too spaced out and, since only a small number can be simultaneously held in the short-term store, it will be harder to recognize relationships and form links. Too broad a presentation can inhibit supersign formation.

2. The flow of didactic information is too large and exceeds the user's intake capacity. In this case not all the relevant elements can be perceived, which consequently inhibits cognitive processes.

Productive Thinking, Creativity. In Gestalt psychology and thought psychology, a series of experiments are quoted to show that the solution of a problem depends on the situation in which the problem is first presented; see Wertheimer (1957). Problem-solving is facilitated if it is achieved through structuring which, again, is effected through the use of frequent and familiar patterns. It is not easy to solve problems when the virtual models leading to the solution have to be structured in an unfamiliar way.

In terms of information theory, this means that solution strategies and patterns have different amounts of information according to the frequency with which they are used. Thus an often used strategy has little information. This is also true of the mental operations required to pursue this strategy. The conscious capacity is not cluttered up with information relating to the strategy. In consequence, the virtual internal models can be more complex if they contain familiar elements and familiar classifying structures.

If the structure of the problem forces the student to use unfamiliar strategies and structures, both the information of the strategy and that of the mental operations required to carry it out are larger and place more strain on the conscious capacity. The complexity of the internal models declines when models have to be structured and organized in an unfamiliar way.

This fact not only explains why more unusual strategies are not immediately applied, it also explains why unfamiliar methods of attack at first lead to less complex models and therefore have an objectively smaller range. The general aim of teaching is to build up an internal repertory of solution strategies, mutual dependences and relationships such that the transinformation of this repertory onto the combined set of all general object fields of the external world is as large as possible. We may therefore conclude that, if education is to encourage creativity and insight into all kinds of problem fields, it must avoid the excessive use of a limited repertory of solution strategies and patterns, because this increases the information of the more unusual strategies and reduces the degrees of freedom for the solution of open problems.

4.5.2   Problem-Oriented Instruction

To favor learning that produces insights in a particular context, some orientation relative to the problems of the subject is necessary before planning a teaching strategy or developing a teaching algorithm. The first and most important phase of teaching is the exposition of the problem and the identification of its components.

Kerschensteiner (1914) proposed an ideal-type form of instruction for the natural sciences which is known in the literature of methodology as "exploratory teaching". Kerschensteiner adapted the process of acquiring new knowledge in the associated sciences of physics and chemistry to learning, by teaching the pupils to solve subjectively unknown problems largely by their own efforts. A form of problem-oriented teaching adapted to technical subject matter is "rediscovery teaching" (Weltner, 1963), where the process of problem-solving for technical purposes is adapted as a teaching strategy. Both forms have the following features:

First Phase of Instruction. A scientific problem or technical exercise is set.

Second Phase of Instruction. The students propose methods of attack and these are discussed. In this phase, the pupils must be allowed adequate time to form internal models. Thus, after he has set the problem, the teacher must not offer the solution too quickly.

Third Phase. The viability of the methods of attack is tested, if necessary by carrying out experiments or building models derived from those methods. This determines the transinformation of the internal models onto the problem field. This phase of verification includes making judgements about the value of the various virtual models.

In science teaching, the criterion of the usefulness of a method of attack is the transinformation onto the objectively existing problem field.

In well-thought-out, problem-oriented teaching, not only the order in which the elements of the subject matter are introduced but also the emphasis given to them in teaching form part of the presentation of the exercise or problem. It is not the facts which are stressed, but rather the relationships between the facts. From the viewpoint of information theory, there are two reasons for recommending problem-oriented teaching:

a) the conditional information of interdependent elements is smaller, so the probability of retention is increased.

b) The relations between elements are operators, valid for classes of elements. Internally formed operators have, in addition to the transinformation onto the particular case, transinformation onto all elements of that category.

4.5.3   Transfer and Transinformation

Transfer, or carrying over, means that in the process of learning about a particular subject other things are learned which can apply to other subjects. There are two classical theories of transfer:

a) Thorndike (1914) thought the reason for transfer between two problem situations was that the same elements occurred within both situations. The basis of the transfer is that there should be "identical elements" in both situations.

b) The rival concept of Judd (1908) held that the possibility of transfer lay in the identity of the relationships between elements in two situations (generalization theory).

Classic Example. Subjects required to throw darts at underwater targets were divided into two groups. The first group had studied optics and knew the law of refraction, the second did not. The water level was lowered in the course of the experiment. The group that knew the law of refraction did better, thus showing transfer.

Seen from the point of view of information theory, the ideas of Thorndike and Judd are coincident. Identical signs are involved in both cases, but Thorndike saw them at the level of elements and Judd at the level of relationships, i.e. supersigns.

Transfer is the transinformation of the internal models of a field of perception or learning onto a new field.

For the theory of education and for the determination of teaching objectives, the important thing is to know which internal models have maximal transinformation onto the fields of perception relevant to a particular subject. By definition this question does not admit of a generalized solution, because perception fields and problem fields are different for different people. The formation of internal models of facts has transinformation only onto these particular facts. Internal models of relationships, problem-solving strategies, internal operators (supersigns of first and second order) have transinformation onto categories. If we consider the external world as a product field of any number of fields, the transinformation of second-order signs is larger.

Transinformation of a Rule Onto a Problem Field. The transinformation of an internally available rule may be equal to the entire information of the problem.

Example. For a student who knows Ohm's law, the amperage resulting from a given voltage and resistance in a copper wire is without information, since he could have worked it out entirely from the given facts.

Frequently the transinformation of the rule onto the problem field is smaller than the information of the field. In such a case, the solution to the problem is not completely given, but at any rate the alternatives have been restricted.

Example. If the AC potential across a coil is known and the ohmic resistance of the coil is also known, a knowledge of Ohm's law is not sufficient to enable the student to determine the amperage. He can, however, determine the maximum amperage which will not be exceeded under any circumstances.

Although the transinformation of the rule onto the problem field does not entirely eliminate its information for the student, it certainly reduces it. This is by far the most frequent case in situations involving problems and decisions. The internal knowledge and available operators have a certain transinformation which restricts the information of the problem fields contained in situations involving problems and decisions but does not completely eliminate it. The exploitation of the maximum possible transinformation onto problem fields is an ultimate objective of all teaching processes.

The optimization of the transinformation from the repertory of internal models onto the product field of the external world is a problem of selection. From the repertory of all internally known rules and laws the student has to select those with maximum transinformation onto the product field. Transinformation is a symmetric relationship. It exists between the problem field and the field of internally available models. In teaching situations this transinformation will usually be larger than in the situations involving problem-solving and decisions for which a general education should prepare the pupil. Nevertheless, the relationship between the two fields should not degenerate to the extreme case where, in the subject being taught, certain problems are always assigned certain definite methods of solution. In this case, restricting the effective repertory gives maximal transinformation with respect to the restricted repertory, but only with respect to that, so that no transfer is effected.

If transinformation in problem-oriented teaching is to be brought up to the level of transinformation required for the total available repertory of methods of attack and general problem fields, the problems set during teaching must be both over- and under-determined. This is the only way to ensure that the transinformation of the problem onto the field of the rules is not identical with the information of the selection.

Our consideration of the transinformation of the problem field onto the field of internal models and problem-solving strategies may now be developed into a theory for measuring achievement of transfer.

Summary. An analysis of the process of teaching and learning from the point of view of information theory yields at the elementary level approaches to a theory of teaching which can be derived from a unified theoretical concept and stated quantitatively.

Learning processes are conceived of as involving the construction of internal models whose transinformation onto the external world and problem fields can be measured empirically. We thus have a link between the concept of information theory and values that can be measured empirically.

The logical relationships within subjects to be taught can be studied by means of coherence structure diagrams. In this way the boundary conditions for different types of subject matter can be determined and teaching algorithms developed. The block-diagram technique may be applied to the analysis of the structure of subjects to be taught and also used as a network plan for the development of curricula.

Finally, a consideration of the cognitive processes involved establishes the link with thought psychology. A study of the transinformation between the external world and problem fields on the one hand and the field of internal models on the other defines the problem of teaching objectives and supplies a criterion for their selection.

5 Use of the Guessing Game to Determine Subjective Information: A Practical Guide

5.1 Selection of Text Sample and Preparation of Experimental Material

It is important when conducting guessing-game experiments to have well-prepared test material, a good technique of administering tests, and a problem-oriented plan. This chapter stresses the organizational details, not because of their theoretical relevance, but because of their practical utility.

5.1.1 Length of Text Samples

Let us assume we have a text and a particular experimental objective. (Examples: transinformation analysis to determine the didactic transinformation, or subjective information, of various texts as a function of the age and existing knowledge of the subjects; information uptake from once-through or repeated reading; memory tests).

The length of the text sample depends on how long each experiment is to last. It has proved valuable to have the subjects work in pairs once they are familiar with the technique of guessing games. This can always be done with students. One partner tests the other and they change roles in the course of the experiment. No undue fatigue was induced with an arrangement where each session allowed for each student to adminster tests for two 15-minute periods and to act as subject for two 15-minute periods. However, when estimating the time required, a deviation of about $\pm 40\%$ can be expected. The roles are reversed after each part of the experiment.

When several sessions are required to complete one experimental plan, it is advisable to make up different pairs in order to avoid any bias in the composition of the groups. The students must be trained for their roles as testers and subjects by practice in the particular technique to be applied. It is important to make it clear that these experiments are not intelligence tests.

When experiments are to be carried out with schoolchildren or with subjects unused to psychological tests, role changing between partners is not feasible and the experiment must be conducted by trained persons appointed for the purpose. In this case, the maximum test duration without symptoms of fatigue will be two 10- to 15-minute periods with a break between.

The times quoted determine the length of the text sample to be used for each part of the experiment, according to the particular guessing procedure. Since the guessing time also depends on the subjective information of the text, a text of average difficulty can be assumed to contain roughly 1.6 bits per sign. Below we give average values for guessing speed in signs per minute, and the number of words predicted in a 15-minute test with an average word length of 7 signs per word.

Guessing with the branching diagram:
 5 signs per minute,
10 words in 15 minutes.

Simplified procedure with letter-by-letter prediction:
10 signs per minute,
20 words in 15 minutes.

Simplified procedure with word-by-word prediction:
40 signs per minute,
80 words in 15 minutes.

5.1.2   Selecting the Sample from the Whole Text

A fundamental distinction must be made between two different situations:

a) It is desired to find the subjective information of certain word groups such as nouns, adjectives, foreign words, technical terms, terminal rhymes in poems, or the way in which the subjective information depends on the position of the word in the sentence, etc.

b) It is desired to find the subjective information of the text as a whole, which can be a function of age, education, previous knowledge, teaching, and other variables. In case a) the choice of text sample depends upon the question to be answered and cannot be treated here in general. In case b) a text sample must be picked at random from the text as a whole. When both the length of the text sample and the length of the whole text are known, several procedures which are equivalent to random methods are available:

a) The text sample is determined word by word in a completely random manner, the words being numbered and those to be guessed being picked at random. These words are predicted in context, the preceding words being known. It is only when measuring the information of scrambled texts that the random sequence of the words is retained. This method is not very easy to operate and its use is recommended only when a very high speed of prediction is sought so that the experiment will simulate information uptake during reading. In this case the appropriate guessing procedure is the prediction of complete words.

b) The same effect is obtained by using the grid procedure in which the words to be guessed are always separated by the same number of words. If, for instance, 30 words are to be guessed from a text of 240 words, every eighth word can be selected. Alternatively, groups of two or more consecutive words may be taken, leaving correspondingly more words between them. Instead of 30 words, each 8 words apart from the next, one might, for instance, select 5 groups of 6 consecutive words, each group being correspondingly farther from the next one. This schematic procedure is adequate in randomness with respect to type of word, word position in the sentence, and similar characteristics, provided the text sample is fairly large. Taking groups of words and applying the grid procedure can considerably simplify the preparation of the material and the conduct of the experiment.

It should really be mandatory that a fairly large experiment is planned, using a number of subjects. This offers the possibility of either including quite large portions of the text in the experiment by moving the grid for different subjects, or having several subjects predict the same samples of text. Which variation is preferred will depend upon the purpose of the experiment.

For instance, one may wish to measure differences in the subjective information as a function of certain variables relative to the subject, or one may wish to measure the subjective information of various text samples for homogeneous groups of subjects.

5.1.3   Technical Preparation of the Experimental Material

Let us say we have a sample of 30 words consisting of five groups of six consecutive words selected from a text having a total of 240 words. The technical problem is this: the subject begins by reading part of the text, then he comes to the six words which he has to predict, then another passage of text for reading, and so on. We found that the method where the test administrator places a piece of paper or cardboard over the words and moves it by hand did not work too well. A much more reliable method is to compile booklets, which are quite quickly produced, where fixed cover sheets are placed over the words to be guessed. Here is a detailed description of how to make up such booklets:

The 240-word text is typed, six words to a line, on to matrices; this can be done by an assistant. Using the grid procedure, one selects from the total of 40 lines five lines, leaving eight lines between each. One can use dice or random-number tables to decide which of the eight lines to begin on. The last line to be guessed on the page is covered with a sheet of white bond letter paper so that the preceding line can be read. The next to last line to be guessed is covered with another sheet of paper in similar fashion, and so on until the first line to be guessed has been covered. The cover sheets are stapled to the left-hand margin to hold them in position. As each line is guessed, the cover sheet is turned over to reveal the next part of the text as far as the next line to be predicted. If the portion of the cover sheets projecting at the bottom is trimmed off, we have a booklet, ready for use, in letter-paper size; the whole may be placed in folder. It takes 3–4 minutes to prepare each booklet.

If the experiment is worked in pairs, a folded sheet with the lines to be guessed underscored is placed in the folder for the tester. We found it worthwhile to add an explanatory note to each folder, setting out the boundary conditions for both parties to the experiment. If an experiment is conducted with several pairs at once, the groups should be unable to hear each other so as to prevent the unintentional transmission of information or the giving of assistance during prediction. Thus, the number of groups that can take part in such an experiment is limited by the number of separate rooms available.

5.1.4 Experimental Design

With larger experiments, it was found practicable when working with students to use groups of 32 to 48 students who form 16 to 24 pairs. This technique allows longer text samples to be analyzed. The problem and experimental design determine the size of the acceptable error relative to the text sample and the deviation within the experimental group. In the experiments we conducted, we arranged for the test to include on average a 20% sample of the complete text.

When working with schoolchildren, we found it necessary to use smaller units, i.e. groups of 12 to 16 children. School classes can be used to form parallel groups.

When carrying out transinformation analysis—memory tests, didactic transinformation, etc.—the experimental design must allow for suitable parallel groups where the only difference between the groups is in the influence of the variable to be investigated. If the subjective information of a text is to be measured, there will necessarily be uptake of information and this in itself will change the conditions for later measurements. When forming parallel groups, children in the same class may be assigned on the basis of such variables as school grades in English or mathematics, or in subjects relevant to the investigation.

If several groups have to be formed for transinformation analysis, care must be taken to ensure that subjects of equivalent ranking predict the same text sample.

If it is not feasible to form parallel groups on the basis of school grades (as when dealing with students or adults), a standard reading test may be given and the result used as a criterion; alternatively, behavior during guessing games may be evaluated. Obviously, the constitution of the parallel groups must always take into account the variables relevant to the experimental design.

5.2   How to Carry out the Experiment: Some Examples

5.2.1   Use of the Branching Diagram

A. Normal Case

The subject has the folder in front of him, and the diagram lies between him and the experimenter. The subject reads the first part of the text up to the beginning of the covered line. He then begins to predict the first letter of the next word, using the branching diagram. He starts from the point at the top of the branching diagram, as shown in Fig. 5.1.

There is a path starting at the top which runs via five branching points to each individual symbol. To help the subject to orient himself, the vowels are on the left, the consonants in the middle and the punctuation marks on the right. The vowels and consonants are arranged alphabetically within their sub-groups. In making his prediction, the subject has to assess the probability of groups of letters and compare two sets of probabilities with each other. Thus, the grouping of the letters must be easy to scan. In relatively many cases the decision "consonant" or "vowel" is strongly dependent on the preceding letter sequence. The branching diagram was devised to take account of this frequent preliminary decision. After this, alphabetical order is used within the sub-groups, as being most familiar to the subject and allowing him the fastest orientation. In this way it is hoped to minimize errors arising from orientation within the diagram.

It has sometimes been suggested that for letter prediction the letters be arranged in order of their relative frequency in the language. The intention here is to place the most frequent symbols together because

Fig. 5.1

on average these are also the most probable. There is a flaw in this argument, however, because the probability of a symbol depends on its position in the text. In German, if we have S and C, H is very likely to follow, quite apart from the overall frequency of H in the language. The subjective probability of any letter in the alphabet depends above all on the context and on the letters that have gone before, much more than on its relative frequency in the language. This probability is a fluctuating one which even changes as the guessing procedure moves along.

The experiment is conducted so that the subject always predicts in context and can suggest reasonable continuations. Here is an example of letter-by-letter prediction of a text sample of six words. The example has been retained in the original German; an English translation is given. The principles on which the conduct and scoring of the guessing game proceed should be clear enough, and they can readily be adapted to the requirements of other languages. The calibration curves were worked out for use with German and must be determined empirically for any other languages to be used. Up to the present there are no calibration curves available for English. Although any necessary corrections would not change the basic course of the curves, they might displace the numerical values. Thus. the calibration curves in the form in which they are given here should be used with other languages only for the purpose of orientation.

The subject knows the preceding text and has already predicted 4 words; 2 words remain to be predicted. The preceding text is printed, and the words already predicted are written in block capitals. (This example is the definition of the entry "Repertoire" in the *Lexikon der Kybernetischen Pädagogik und der Programmierten Instruktion*, Schnelle, Quickborn – Hamburg, 1967):

Ein endliches Repertoire ist eine endliche Menge von Möglichkeiten, von denen in
JEDER SITUATION GENAU EINE[5]

(A finite repertory is a finite set of possibilities of which in EACH SITUATION JUST ONE...)

The subject must predict the continuation. From the context, he could expect a number of possible continuations:

EINZIGE SICH EREIGNET	(single one happens)
REALISIERT WIRD	(is realized)
WAHRGENOMMEN WERDEN KANN	(can be perceived)
WIRKLICHKEIT WIRD	(becomes reality)

[5] Because the use of upper and lower case letters has grammatical significance in German, all predicted letters are witten as capitals.

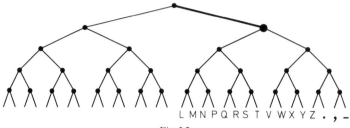

L M N P Q R S T V W X Y Z . , _

Fig. 5.2

all of which would make sense within the context. The subject may think the first continuation more likely than the other three: E is reached via the left branch, R and W via the right branch; therefore he would say "left" at the first decision point. The prediction is false, and the tester says, "right is correct", pointing to the next decision point from which prediction will proceed for a restricted repertoire; see Fig. 5.2.

Of the remaining continuations

REALISIERT WIRD
WAHRGENOMMEN WERDEN KANN
WIRKLICHKEIT WIRD

the subject thinks REALISIERT WIRD the most likely and says "left". This prediction too is false, and the tester says, "right is correct", thus providing help for the second time, and points to the next decision point. From here prediction proceeds with a still more restricted repertoire; see Fig. 5.3. Since both remaining continuations begin with W

WAHRGENOMMEN WERDEN KANN
WIRKLICHKEIT WIRD,

the subject says "right", which is, of course, correct. The tester says "right is correct" and points to the next decision point; see Fig. 5.4.

The next two predictions from that decision point, first "left", then "right" again, are also correct. The tester now writes down following the preceding text the letter just predicted and below it on the cover sheet notes the number of incorrect predictions.

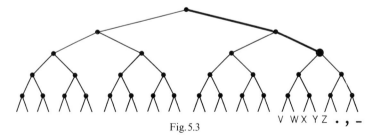

V W X Y Z . , _

Fig. 5.3

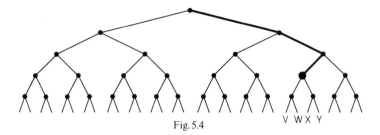

Fig. 5.4

V W X Y

Prediction of the next letter again starts at the first decision point of the diagram.

Ein endliches Repertoire ist eine endliche Menge von Möglichkeiten, von denen in
JEDER SITUATION GENAU EINE W   2

B. Special Case

A particular letter is expected with high probability. In this case it is admissible to predict the letter immediately. This is justified on theoretical grounds because the subjective probability of a letter occurring is more than 0.5 and the summed probability for all the other letters is less than 0.5 If this is the case, it is obvious that at every decision point in the diagram, from start to finish, the alternative which leads to that letter will be selected.

Let us assume this to be the case in our example for the expectation of the continuation:

WAHRGENOMMEN WERDEN KANN

The subject says, "with high probability, A". This predicts the path through the branching diagram. If the path is entirely correct, the tester will say "correct" and will write the letter on the cover sheet. But if the

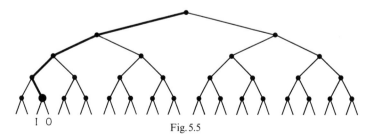

I O

Fig. 5.5

prediction is not correct, the path through the branching diagram will be scored as correct to the extent that it leads to the correct letter. The tester then indicates the decision point up to which the path selected by the predicted letter was correct and from which prediction must now proceed; see Fig. 5.5

At this point, the subject predicts on the basis of his one remaining alternative,

WIRKLICHKEIT WIRD

and says "I".

The prediction is correct. I is written on the cover sheet and a note made underneath it that one mistake was made.

Ein endliches Repertoire ist eine endliche Menge von Möglichkeiten, von denen in

---

JEDER SITUATION GENAU EINE WI
21

C. Special Case

A sequence of letters is expected with high probability. In our example the subject expects with great certainty the continutation

WIRKLICHKEIT WIRD

and considers any other continuation subjectively very unlikely.

When a case occurs in which a sequence of letters, a word or a sequence of words is expected with high probability, then the entire word or the entire sequence can be predicted as a whole. Theoretically this is justified, provided the expectation probability for each letter in the sequence exceeds 0.5. This occurs rarely at the beginning of a word, but more frequently at the end of a word and in longer words. In the instance under consideration, the subject would say: "With very high probability the sequence – WIRKLICHKEIT WIRD". If the predicted sequence of letters, or the word, or the sequence of words is correct, it is written in block capitals on the cover sheet.

If only part of the letter sequence is correct, the correctly predicted letters will be written down and prediction with the branching diagram will start again with the first incorrectly predicted letter. The new prediction starts at the branching point following the first wrong decision.

In this manner rapid prediction is effected for subjectively information-poor parts of the text and the subject is able to retain the context to a great extent. The procedure is thereby accelerated and the conditions in which the subject predicts are improved. At the same time, errors which could arise from mistakes in perceiving the path through the branching point labyrinth are reduced.

If the subject predicts the complete line, the cover sheet is simply turned over, revealing the text leading up to the next line to be predicted.

Thus, when the experiment is finished, the folder contains a complete experimental protocol in the shape of the results written on the cover sheets. The cover sheets may also record the name of subject and the tester, and such additional data as time of day, duration of experiment, etc.

Here is an example of how one line is scored. In reality the entire text sample would consist of several lines.

Ein endliches Repertoire ist eine endliche
Menge von Möglichkeiten. von denen in

JEDER SITUATION GENAU EINE WIRKLICHKEIT WIRD
31   311   322   2   21

Scoring:

Number of letters	45
Number of wrong guesses	22
Number of branching points	$5 \times 45 = 225$
Average number of mistakes per branching point	0.098
Average information per branching point, calibration curve (1)	0.33 bits
Average information per letter	1.65 bits/sign
Information of the text sample	74 bits

Mixed Repertory. When dealing with mixed repertories including letters, numbers, and symbols, each repertory must be scored separately.

The scoring then differs from the example given above for letters: the number to be inserted under *number of branching points* is the number of decisions needed to go from the starting point to the element of the repertory, not, as above, the five decisions required in the letter repertory.

5.2.2   Simplified Procedure (1): Prediction by Letters

The subject makes one prediction attempt for each letter, after which the tester immediately tells him the correct letter, writes it in block letters on the cover sheet and underlines it if it was wrong.

In this case the experiment would proceed as follows:

Assume that the alternatives which occur to the subject are the same. He predicts the most likely of the alternatives, namely E. The tester tells him that E is incorrect and W is correct; he writes down W and the subject proceeds to to the next prediction, now calling out A. The tester says, "wrong, I is correct" and writes down I. The next prediction is R, which is correct. If now the entire word is predicted, it will be written down at once

---

Ein endliches Repertoire ist eine endliche
Menge von Möglichkeiten, von denen in

JEDER SITUATION GENAU EINE WIRKLICHKEIT WIRD

`,,`   `,,,`   `,,,`   `,,`

Scoring:

Number of letters 45
Number of wrong guesses 12
Ratio of wrong guesses to letters 0.267
Average information per letter, calibration curve (2) ... 1.67 bits/sign
Information of the entire text sample....................... 75 bits

5.2.3   Simplified Procedure (2): Prediction by Syllables

The subject makes one prediction attempt for each syllable, after which the tester immediately tells him the correct syllable, writes it on the cover sheet and underlines it if it was wrong.

Ein endliches Repertoire ist eine endliche
Menge von Möglichkeiten, von denen in

JEDER SITUATION GENAU EINE WIRKLICHKEIT WIRD

— —   — —   — —   —   —

Scoring:

Number of syllables 14
Number of wrong guesses 8
Ratio of wrong guesses to syllables 0.57
Information per syllable, calibration curve (3) ...... 6.1 bits/syllable
Information per letter .... 1.90 bits/sign
Information of text sample 85   bits

5.2.4   Simplified Procedure (3): Prediction by Words

Here the subject makes one prediction for each word, after which the tester tells him the correct word and writes it on the cover sheet, underlined if wrong, and goes on to the next word. It should be noted here that, if the text sample is small, the deviation may be large.

Ein endliches Repertoire ist eine endliche
Menge von Möglichkeiten, von denen in

JEDER SITUATION GENAU EINE WIRKLICHKEIT WIRD

Scoring:

Number of words	6
Number of wrong guesses	5
Wrong guesses per word	0.833
Information per word, calibration curve (4)	13.3
Information per letter	1.77 bit/sign
Information of text sample	80.0 bits

The percentage of wrongly guessed words for ordinary texts is 70% to 90%. The subjects are more often wrong than right and sometimes become discouraged. Therefore we found it useful to warn subjects in such experiments that a high proportion of incorrect predictions is normal and to be expected, and that $20\% - 30\%$ of correct guesses is a very good performance. The same text sample was used in all of the above examples. The differences in the information of the text sample obtained by the four procedures are random errors because the sample is so small.

5.3   Special Problems in Conducting the Experiments

Punctuation and Ends of Words. A great deal of thought has been given to the handling of ends of words and punctuation marks in this investigation. To be consistent, one should use the same technique for ends of words and punctuation marks, as against letters, as is used for determining the subjective information with a mixed repertory. Letters, punctuation marks and word spacers belong to different repertories and are perceived as different repertories. This argument is balanced by the desire to keep the machinery of the experiment as simple and clear as possible, since anyway it makes demands on the subject which distract him from the real problem. This is why, in most experiments, word spacers, periods and commas are included in the repertory of signs which make up a text, and not treated as separate repertories of letters and punctuation marks.

To make the procedure simpler for the subject, who sometimes fails to predict word spacers or punctuation marks merely because he thinks it trivial, we proceeded as follows:

a) The subject calls a complete word or, if he predicted the initial letters of a word incorrectly, the remainder of the word in one prediction. In such a case the end of the word is counted as predicted. If a punctuation mark follows and not the end of the word, the decision points below the one between word end and punctuation mark will be counted as correctly predicted, and the subject will proceed to predict the punctuation mark.

b) Prediction of a punctuation mark implies the end of the word.

c) The subject predicts part of a word, but not all of it. From the first letter not predicted, the procedure then goes on in normal fashion.

d) The subject predicts a complete word, but it is longer than the word sought. For instance, if the word to be predicted is STATION, the subject might say STATIONMASTER. In such a case, the tester writes down STATION and proceeds in normal fashion to the prediction of the word spacer (end of word).

Special Signs. Any text may contain special signs, numbers and other symbols. If these are present in significant numbers, the procedure for the determination of subjective information with a mixed repertory has to be used (Section 2.6). If the special signs are relatively few, one may have to accept a deliberate falsification and rewrite the text. Then signs such as apostrophe "s", exclamation mark, etc., which are not included in the repertory must be replaced by periods or commas. Subjects will be told that where special signs are expected, commas or periods should be predicted according to the sense. Other special symbols will not be included in prediction and scoring and will be given straight away by the tester as necessary.

Example. The text contains the date "1914". The tester will write down 1914 without any guessing and leave it out of the letter or word count.

Where such a rewriting or omission is made, it must always be noted because it is precisely when mixed repertories are involved that the subjective information of the entire sign sequence rises.

Small Letters and Capitals. Except when investigating the influence of small and capital letters, no attempt was made in the experiments to distinguish between them (see note on p. 65). The tester always wrote the predicted letters as capitals during an experiment. This simplification, whose importance is much greater for the German language, may have made the measured subjective information too low. The investigations described in Chapter 2 show that the systematic experimental error is of the order of 2 %.

5.4   Guessing Games Using Computers with Typewriters as Input and Output Units

The measurement of the subjective information of texts and sign sequences may be carried out independently of the tester by having the text

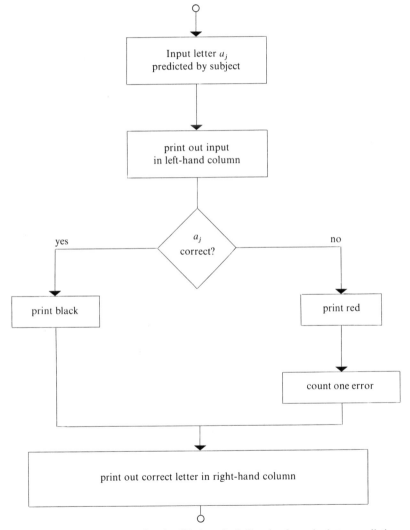

Fig. 5.6. Part of flow diagram for simplified method (1) using letter-by-letter prediction.

predicted by means of a computer-controlled typewriter. The subject conveys his predictions to the computer via the typewriter keyboard. The computer can be programmed to print out the correct continuation (letters, syllables, words) when a simplified procedure is used, printing correct predictions in black and incorrect predictions in red. If a branching diagram is used, the repertory still available for the continuation can be printed out after each decision.

We were even able to determine the subjective information of pictures with the aid of a N 820 Nixdorf computer, the subject predicting the tone value *black* or *white* for each picture dot. Scanning of picture dots was done line by line.

The advantage of such a procedure is that it eliminates errors due to unconscious communication between subject and tester. However, control experiments carried out to date show no significant difference between experiments where students act as testers and those carried out with the aid of computers. The use of computers allows in addition immediate quantitative evaluation of test results.

Fig. 5.6 shows part of a flow diagram used for determining subjective information by the simplified method of letter-by-letter prediction; see Weltner & Heinrich, 1969.

5.5   Tables and Graphs

5.5.1   How to Use the Tables

a) The tables are accurate enough for almost all purposes likely to arise. Columns 2−6 are taken from the tables published by Frank (1969); his tables should be used if greater accuracy is required.

b) In many empirical determinations of the average information of events, it is simpler to avoid having to calculate the relative frequencies

$$h_k = \frac{N_k}{N} \approx p_k$$

by resorting to the formula

$$H = \sum_{K=1}^{r} p_k \operatorname{ld} \frac{1}{p_k} = \frac{1}{N} \left[N \operatorname{ld} N - \sum_{K=1}^{r} N_k \operatorname{ld} N_k \right]$$

since the N_k are empirically given and H can then easily be found.

Column (1) lists N and p as percentages.

For $1 < N_k < 100$, $N_k \operatorname{ld} N_k$ may be read off directly from column (3).

c) When empirical prediction experiments using branching diagrams are carried out, column (7) shows the best estimate currently available of H_{sub} per branching point.

5.5.2   How to Use the Graphs

a) For rough calculations, diagrams 1 and 2 give the curves for

$$\mathrm{ld}\,\frac{1}{p}, \; p\,\mathrm{ld}\,\frac{1}{p}$$

and the values may be read off directly. H_{sub} in diagram 3 allows determination of subjective information by means of the branching diagram.

b) Three calibration curves are shown in diagrams 4, 5, and 6 for the empirical determination of subjective information by the simplified procedures. First we determine empirically the ratio of incorrectly predicted letters (or syllables, or words). For procedure (1), we need the ratio of letters incorrectly predicted at the first attempt:

$$C_{\mathrm{letters}} = \frac{N_{\mathrm{letters,\,F}}}{N_{\mathrm{letters}}}.$$

For procedure (2), we need the ratio of syllables incorrectly predicted at the first attempt:

$$C_{\mathrm{syllables}} = \frac{N_{\mathrm{syllables,\,F}}}{N_{\mathrm{syllables}}}$$

and for procedure (3) the ratio of words incorrectly predicted at the first attempt:

$$C_{\mathrm{words}} = \frac{N_{\mathrm{words,\,F}}}{N_{\mathrm{words}}}$$

H_{sub} may then be read off directly for whichever unit was used for prediction. If, for instance, we are using simplified procedure (3) where words are predicted, we obtain H_{sub} per word. If we also wish to know H_{sub} per letter, then a separate calculation must be carried out, dividing by the average number of letters per word.

1	2	3	4	5	6	7
$\dfrac{N}{p\,(\%)}$	$\operatorname{ld} N$	$N \operatorname{ld} N$	$\operatorname{ld} \dfrac{1}{p}$	$p \operatorname{ld} \dfrac{1}{p}$	$h = p \operatorname{ld} \dfrac{1}{p}$ $+ (1-p) \operatorname{ld} \dfrac{1}{1-p}$	$H_{\text{sub}}(p)$ $= \dfrac{2p+h}{2}$
0	$-\infty$	0	∞	0	0	0
1	0.0000	0.00	6.6439	0.0664	0.0808	0.0504
2	1.0000	2.00	5.6439	0.1129	0.1414	0.0907
3	1.5850	4.75	5.0589	0.1518	0.1944	0.1272
4	2.0000	8.00	4.6439	0.1856	0.2423	0.1612
5	2.3219	11.61	4.3219	0.2161	0.2864	0.1932
6	2.5859	15.51	4.0589	0.2435	0.3274	0.2237
7	2.8074	19.65	3.8365	0.2686	0.3659	0.2530
8	3.0000	24.00	3.6439	0.2915	0.4022	0.2811
9	3.1699	28.53	3.4739	0.3127	0.4365	0.3082
10	3.3219	33.22	3.3219	0.3322	0.4690	0.3345
11	3.4594	38.05	3.1844	0.3503	0.4999	0.3510
12	3.5850	43.02	3.0589	0.3671	0.5294	0.3847
13	3.7004	48.11	2.9434	0.3826	0.5574	0.4087
14	3.8074	53.30	2.8365	0.3971	0.5842	0.4321
15	3.9069	58.60	2.7370	0.4105	0.6098	0.4549
16	4.0000	64.00	2.6439	0.4230	0.6343	0.4772
17	4.0875	69.49	2.5564	0.4346	0.6577	0.4989
18	4.1699	75.06	2.4739	0.4453	0.6801	0.5201
19	4.2479	80.71	2.3959	0.4552	0.7015	0.5408
20	4.3219	86.44	2.3219	0.4644	0.7219	0.5610
21	4.3923	92.24	2.2515	0.4728	0.7415	0.5808
22	4.4594	98.11	2.1844	0.4806	0.7602	0.6061
23	4.5236	104.04	2.1203	0.4877	0.7780	0.6190
24	4.5850	110.04	2.0589	0.4941	0.7950	0.6375
25	4.6439	116.10	2.0000	0.5000	0.8113	0.6556
26	4.7004	122.21	1.9434	0.5053	0.8267	0.6734
27	4.7549	128.38	1.8890	0.5100	0.8415	0.6908
28	4.8074	134.61	1.8365	0.5142	0.8555	0.7678
29	4.8580	140.88	1.7909	0.5176	0.8687	0.7237
30	4.9069	147.21	1.7370	0.5211	0.8813	0.7407
31	4.9542	153.58	1.6897	0.5238	0.8932	0.7566
32	5.0000	160.00	1.6439	0.5260	0.9044	0.7722
33	5.0444	166.47	1.5995	0.5278	0.9149	0.7875
34	5.0875	172.97	1.5564	0.5292	0.9248	0.8024
35	5.1293	179.52	1.5146	0.5301	0.9341	0.8171
36	5.1699	186.12	1.4739	0.5306	0.9427	0.8314
37	5.2095	192.75	1.4344	0.5307	0.9507	0.8454
38	5.2479	199.42	1.3959	0.5305	0.9580	0.8590
39	5.2854	206.13	1.3585	0.5298	0.9648	0.8724
40	5.3219	212.88	1.3219	0.5288	0.9710	0.8855
41	5.3576	219.66	1.2863	0.5274	0.9765	0.8983
42	5.3923	226.48	1.2515	0.5256	0.9815	0.9108
43	5.4263	233.33	1.2176	0.5236	0.9858	0.9229
44	5.4594	240.21	1.1844	0.5211	0.9896	0.9348
45	5.4919	247.13	1.1520	0.5184	0.9928	0.9464
46	5.5236	254.08	1.1203	0.5153	0.9954	0.9577
47	5.5546	261.07	1.0893	0.5120	0.9974	0.9687
48	5.5850	268.08	1.0589	0.5083	0.9988	0.9794
49	5.6147	275.12	1.0291	0.5043	0.9997	0.9899

1	2	3	4	5	6
N $p\,(\%)$	$\mathrm{ld}\,N$	$N\,\mathrm{ld}\,N$	$\mathrm{ld}\,\dfrac{1}{p}$	$p\,\mathrm{ld}\,\dfrac{1}{p}$	$h = p\,\mathrm{ld}\,\dfrac{1}{p}$ $+ (1-p)\,\mathrm{ld}\,\dfrac{1}{-p}$
50	5.6439	282.19	1.0000	0.5000	1.0000
51	5.6724	298.29	0.9714	0.4954	0.9997
52	5.7004	296.42	0.9434	0.4906	0.9988
53	5.7279	303.58	0.9159	0.4854	0.9974
54	5.7549	310.76	0.8890	0.4800	0.9954
55	5.7814	317.97	0.8625	0.4744	0.9928
56	5.8074	325.21	0.8365	0.4684	0.9896
57	5.8329	332.47	0.8110	0.4623	0.9858
58	5.8580	339.76	0.7859	0.4558	0.9815
59	5.8826	347.08	0.7612	0.4491	0.9765
60	5.9069	354.41	0.7370	0.4422	0.9710
61	5.9307	361.77	0.7131	0.4350	0.9648
62	5.9542	369.16	0.6897	0.4276	0.9580
63	5.9773	376.57	0.6666	0.4199	0.9507
64	6.0000	384.00	0.6439	0.4121	0.9427
65	6.0224	391.45	0.6215	0.4040	0.9341
66	6.0444	398.93	0.5995	0.3956	0.9248
67	6.0661	406.43	0.5778	0.3871	0.9149
68	6.0875	413.95	0.5564	0.3783	0.9044
69	6.1085	421.49	0.5353	0.3694	0.8932
70	6.1293	429.05	0.5146	0.3602	0.8813
71	6.1497	436.63	0.4941	0.3508	0.8687
72	6.1699	444.23	0.4739	0.3412	0.8555
73	6.1898	451.86	0.4540	0.3314	0.8415
74	6.2095	459.50	0.4344	0.3215	0.8267
75	6.2288	467.16	0.4150	0.3113	0.8113
76	6.2479	474.84	0.3959	0.3009	0.7950
77	6.2668	482.54	0.3770	0.2903	0.7780
78	6.2854	490.26	0.3584	0.2796	0.7602
79	6.3038	498.00	0.3401	0.2687	0.7415
80	6.3219	505.75	0.3219	0.2575	0.7219
81	6.3399	513.53	0.3040	0.2462	0.7015
82	6.3576	521.32	0.2863	0.2348	0.6801
83	6.3750	529.13	0.2688	0.2231	0.6577
84	6.3923	536.95	0.2515	0.2113	0.6343
85	6.4094	544.80	0.2345	0.1993	0.6098
86	6.4263	552.66	0.2176	0.1871	0.5842
87	6.4429	560.54	0.2009	0.1748	0.5574
88	6.4594	568.43	0.1844	0.1623	0.5294
89	6.4757	576.34	0.1681	0.1496	0.4999
90	6.4919	584.27	0.1520	0.1368	0.4690
91	6.5078	592.21	0.1361	0.1238	0.4365
92	6.5236	600.17	0.1203	0.1107	0.4022
93	6.5392	608.14	0.1047	0.0974	0.3659
94	6.5546	616.13	0.0893	0.0839	0.3274
95	6.5699	624.14	0.0740	0.0703	0.2864
96	6.5850	632.16	0.0589	0.0565	0.2423
97	6.5999	640.19	0.0439	0.0426	0.1944
98	6.6147	648.24	0.0291	0.0286	0.1414
99	6.6294	656.31	0.0145	0.0144	0.0808
100	6.6439	664.39	0.0000	0.0000	0.0000

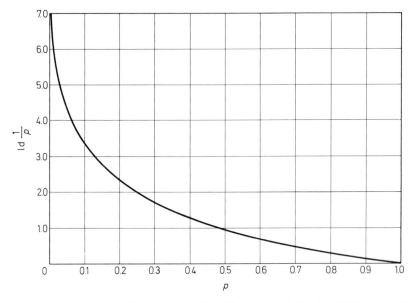

Fig. 5.7   Diagram 1: graphical representation of the function. f $(p) = \mathrm{ld}(1/p)$, for $0 < p \le 1$.

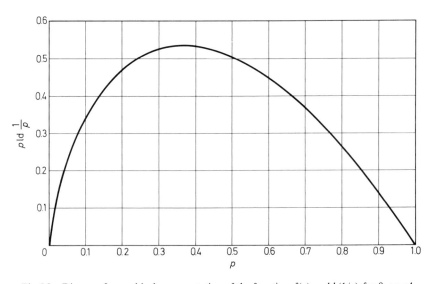

Fig. 5.8   Diagram 2: graphical representation of the function, $f(p) = p\,\mathrm{ld}\,(1/p)$, for $0 \le p \le 1$.

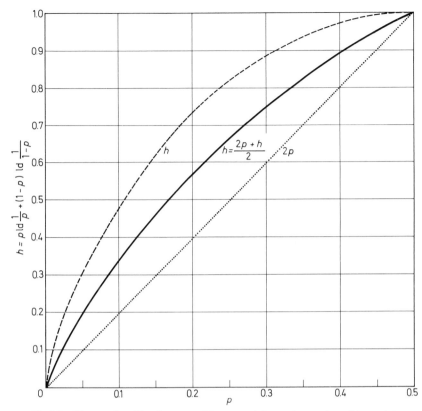

Fig. 5.9 Diagram 3: calibration curve (1): average information per branching point.
— — upper limit; · · · lower limit.

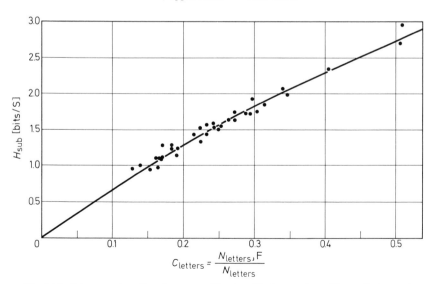

Fig. 5.10 Diagram 4: calibration curve (2): simplified procedure (1), prediction units: words.

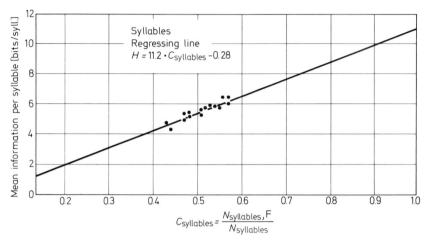

Fig. 5.11   Diagram 5: calibration curve (3): simplified procedure (2), prediction units: syllables.

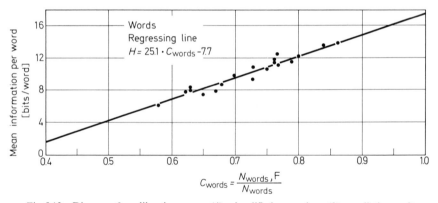

Fig. 5.12   Diagram 6: calibration curve (4): simplified procedure (3), prediction units: words.

Appendix. Notes

2/1. Initially it had been supposed that the eyes glide fairly evenly along the lines during the reading process; now, however, it has been established that eye movement is saccadic and that fixation persists for the greater part of reading time. Further, at subjectively difficult parts of a text, regressions to previous fixation points are observed. According to Schmidt's investigations, for a standardized line of 90 mm and for silent reading, there are 4.1 to 10.8 fixations per line, and for reading aloud 6.1 to 11.5 fixations per line. This indicates that during reading it is not individual words but word sequences that are simultaneously perceived. Further, Erdman, Dodge and Woodworth have shown that when the eye is moving rapidly from one fixation point to the next, recognition of word symbols is practically impossible; see also Gray (1925) and Gray and Rogers (1956).

As early as 1912 Huey observed that apperception during reading occurs in word sequences, words or letters, and that it takes place according to individual needs. Reading is thus a process with controlled repertory change. The decisive criterion is the subjective information of the words or word sequences.

2/2. These calculations are based on the empirically determined law of Estoup (1916) and Zipf (1949) and expressed in the form given by Mandelbrot. This does not take into account that the word sequence in language texts is restricted by the grammatical coherence of that language. An arbitrary sequence of words in a given language does not necessarily form a sentence. This constraint further reduces the information of texts. If words are regarded as supersigns, the conditional frequencies for n-gram dependency may be obtained. In practice this involves considerable expenditure of effort, since even for the determination of bigram dependencies the number of possible bigrams is equal to the square of the words used in the language. Therefore it is virtually impossible to make a statistical analysis of long word sequences. We can only assume for the time being that the decrease in mean information per letter when one switches to the information of letters within words is of the same order of magnitude as the subsequent decrease when one switches to letters within word sequences which are subject to the grammatical constraints.

2/3. To assume that relative frequency is equal to expectation probability implies both the practical problem of measuring errors and the theoretical problem of the concept of probability on which the assumption is based. If we take here the conditional probabilities of the alternatives based on all previous knowledge of the situation by the subject as the expectation probabilities, and use them for the determination of empirical boundary values, there is a contradiction in principle but not in practice with the axiomatic definition of probability; see Peters (1967, pp. 46, 89); Richter (1956).

2/4. The defined probabilities of error of the interval limits are first used here simply to allow grouping and summarization of the empirically obtained entries in the test sheets. This does not make available the interval limits of the decisions so summarized. It can only be said that the true interval limits must lie between the empirically determined averages of neighboring intervals. The average value of p_k for an interval k is empirically determined, but the true limits of the interval are not known. The position of the actual boundary is, however, limited by the average values of the empirical probabilities of error for the neighboring intervals, p_{k-1} and p_{k+1}.

2/5. Kolmogorov succeeded in lowering the upper limit for Shannon's guessing-game method. The experiments were carried out with Russian literature, and the subjects could make predictions as follows (see Jaglom and Jaglom, 1967, p. 216).

1. The next letter will certainly be a particular letter of the alphabet (let us say the k'th).

2. The next letter will certainly be one of two or three letters of the alphabet to be predicted by the subject.

3. The next letter will probably (but not certainly) be a particular letter of the alphabet (say the k'th).

4. The next letter will probably be one of two or three letters to be predicted by the subject.

5. The subject may also say that he has no idea what the following letter will be.

If the predictions are recorded separately according to these criteria, an upper limit may be set for Shannon's method. See Jaglom and Jaglom (1967) for the scoring of the data obtained by means of this procedure. For prediction according to 2. or 4. above, equally likely alternatives were assumed to exist. See Weltner (1967) for prediction experiments using this procedure for German texts. This approach does not permit the lower limit to be raised.

2/6. Sample computation of the narrower limits of subjective information.

If the results on the test data sheet described in Section 2.5.2 are combined into five intervals, one obtains (see also Fig. 2.13)

k	1	2	3	4	5
N_{Fk}	2	2	10	8	26
N_k	247	43	101	40	69
p_k	0.008	0.046	0.099	0.200	0.377

According to Table 5.1, column 6, or from the upper limit of Diagram 3, an h_k corresponding to every p_k may be read off. This yields the upper limit for the k'th interval:

$$I_{k,\,max} = N_k \cdot h_k \quad (2\text{--}43); \qquad I_{max} = \sum_{K=1}^{5} I_{k,\,max} \qquad (2\text{--}44)$$

and for the lower limit:

$$I_{k,min} = N_{1,\,k} \cdot h_{k-1} + N_{2,\,k} \cdot h_{k+1}, \qquad (2\text{--}40)$$

$$I_{min} = \sum_{K=1}^{5} I_{k,\,min} \qquad (2\text{--}41)$$

Computation of the lower limit involves splitting N_k into two terms, $N_{1,k}$ and $N_{2,k}$; see (2–38) and (2–39). Because $I_{k,\,min} = N_{1,k} + N_{2,k} \cdot h_{k+1}$, (2–40), the terms $N_{1,k}$ and $N_{2,k}$ are placed on lines 6 and 7 so that they may always be multipled by h_k for each column. Then $N_k^* = N_{1,k+1} + N_{2,k-1}$ yields $I_{k,\,min} = N_k^* \cdot h_k$. An overview is provided by the table below.

k		Interval						Sum
		1	2	3	4	5		
1	N_{Fk}	2	2	10	8	26		48
2	N_k	247	43	101	40	69		500
3	p_k	0.008	0.046	0.099	0.200	0.377		
4	h_k	0.07	0.27	0.465	0.72	0.955	1	
5	$I_{k,\,max}$	17	12	47	29	66		171
6	$N_{1,\,k+1}$	25	66	25.5	28			
7	$N_{2,\,k-1}$		43	18	35	14.5	41	
8	N_k^*	25	109	43.5	63	14.5	41	
9	$I_{k,\,min}$	2	29	20	45	14	41	151

$I_{min} = 151$ bits; $I_{max} = 171$ bits;
H_{min} (branch) $= 0.30$ bits; H_{max} (branch) $= 0.34$ bits;
H_{min} (letter) $= 1.51$ bits; H_{max} (letter) $= 1.74$ bits.
The initial limits were
H_{min} (letter) $= 0.96$ bits; H_{max} (letter) $= 2.30$ bits.

2/7. When selecting the intervals for the data sheets on which the empirical results of the determined subjective error probabilities are recorded, some arbitrariness will be inevitable. Too fine a division of intervals is pointless because the subjects can only distinguish four to seven effective intervals. A necessary assumption for the computation is that the subjective probabilities of the alternative decisions combined within one interval lie within the boundaries defined by the average values of the neighboring intervals. Errors in assigning individual decisions to particular intervals will invalidate this assumption in proportion to the closeness of the intervals to each other. There are two principles that can be applied when determining interval divisions:

A) from interval boundary to interval boundary the subjective error probabilities are in a constant ratio with respect to one another;

B) from interval boundary to interval boundary the information falls by equal amounts.

The results of four test data sheets were recorded for both principles of sub-division and were evaluated separately. In addition, the number of intervals was varied in order to determine the influence of interval size.

Principle A: A_1) 8 intervals: the error probabilities are in a ratio of $1:2$ for the interval boundaries.

A_2) 4 intervals: error probabilities are as $1:4$.
A_3) 2 intervals: error probabilities are as $1:8$.

Principle B: B_1) 8 intervals: the information difference between interval boundaries is 0.125 bit.

B_2) 4 intervals: the information difference is 0.25 bit.
B_3) 2 intervals: the information difference is 0.5 bit.

There is one interval where the two subdivision principles overlap and this gives the initial boundaries. The figure below shows the result of the computation. The lower and upper boundaries approach asymptotically the dotted line representing the average value of the initial boundaries. Thus subdivision into four intervals provides sufficient convergence. The alternative principles of subdivision have little effect. However, procedure B seems to give faster convergence. For our evalutions, procedure B was used with five intervals.

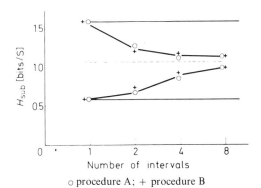

o procedure A; + procedure B

2/8. Table. Subjective information of various texts

Text	No. of signs in sample	No. of subjects	[bit/sign]		
			H_{sub}	σ	σ_M
Scrambled text	274	32	2.88		
Poem (G. v. Vring: Dorf bei Nacht)	218	32	2.14	0.50	0.09
J. Derbolav: "Versuch einer wiss. Grundlegung der Didaktik". In: "Zeitschrift für Pädagogik" 2. Beiheft 1960	1440	12	1.93		
Short story (C. Zuckmayer: "Die Geschichte vom Tümpel")	280	38	1.89		
Prose text (E. Kästner: "Nordafrikanische Wüste")	299	12	1.78		
Rhein. Merkur (column: "Streik gegen den Staat"; 24. 11. 1967)	2091	16	1.71		
Die Zeit (column: "Ostpolitik mit de Gaulle")	2208	30	1.70		
Text from Der Spiegel ("Bombe am Bauch"; 6. 6. 1966)	1250	8	1.70	0.34	0.12
("Riesen am Rande"; 3/1964)	2200	8	1.68	0.50	0.18
Chemistry book text (Henniger-Franck: Chemiebuch für Realschulen, IX A 1957 and Cuny: "Grundlagen der Chemie", 1966)	3629	28	1.65		
Physics book text (R. W. Pohl: Bd. 1, Mechanik, Akustik, Wärmelehre, Berlin 1955, § 74)	2793	16	1.64		
Text from Der Spiegel ("Meerwasserentsalzung", 33/1961)	1480	8	1.64	0.35	0.12
Short story (M. Anger: "Die heimliche Verlobung")	271	40	1.55	0.55	0.09
Novel ("Mein Vaterhaus am Birkenhain")	800	48	1.42	0.47	0.07
Prose text (W. Catelmann: "Der Tierquäler")	389	12	1.27		
Die Zeit (Biography: "Starker Mann am Kongo")	685	10	1.24		
Teaching programs K. Weltner: Physical Forces (experimental version)	1950	16	1.17		
The Four-Stroke Engine (experimental)	6325	16	1.00	0.33	0.09
Heat (experimental)	2527	16	0.97		

2/9. Table. Age dependence of subjective information

text	H_{sub} (bit/S)						Students
	Realschulklasse						
	5	6	7	8	9	10	
A	2.80	2.32	2.34	2.18	2.34	1.84	1.65
	3.30	2.48	2.26	2.54	2.10	2.00	
B	1.72	1.58	1.46	1.38	1.06	1.48	1.17
	1.82	2.04	1.62	1.38	1.49	1.30	

Variance analysis: overall result

Variation	sum of squares	df	mean square	F
between texts	2.80	1	2.80	5.1
between grades	1.25	5	0.25	5.0
texts × grades	0.13	5	0.026	
within	0.61	12	0.05	
total	4.79	23		

List of texts:
Text A: W. Catelmann: "Der Tierquäler" (no. of signs $S = 1269$, sample $= 389$ signs).
Text B: E. Kästner: "Nordafrikanische Wüste". In: "Die Fackel", Band IV, Göttingen, Lesebuch, 8. Schuljahr (no. of signs $S = 1852$, sample $= 299$ signs).

2/10. Table of the subjective information of a mixed repertory

Text	No. of signs				N_{Vp}	[bit/s]					
	text		sample			$H_{letters}$	σ_M	H_{symb}	σ_M	weighted	diff.
	letters	symb	letters	symb		(letters)		(symb)		average	
A_1	6293	648	3119	345	14	1.48	0.06	3.42	0.20	1.67	0.21
B_1	5669	337	3097	289	14	1.49	0.06	2.44	0.34	1.57	0.35
C_1	5460	402	3088	281	14	2.04	0.06	4.20	0.24	2.22	0.25
A_2	1648	213	193	49	14	1.42	0.08	3.64	0.25	1.87	0.26
B_2	1747	125	159	84	14	1.69	0.11	2.65	0.28	2.02	0.32
C_2	1457	188	154	49	12	1.38	0.11	3.24	0.41	1.83	0.42

List of texts:
A: Exercise from mathematics book.
A_1: Breidenbach et al., "Welt der Zahlen". 9th year. Hannover 1965.
A_2: Breidenbach-Kielhorn, "Mathematik", vols. 4. 5 (8th-9th year), Brunswick, 1963-4.
B: Chemistry book text.
B_1: Henniger-Franck, "Chemiebuch für Realschulen", IX A 1957, Stuttgart.
B_2: Cuny, "Grundlagen der Chemie", lst ed., Hann. 1966;
C: Business text from newspapers.
C_1: "Süddeutsche Zeitung", 30 November 1967, business news.
C_2: "Der Tagesspiegel", Berlin, 20 February 1968, business section.
The difference between the subjective information of the letters, H_{ltr}, and of the symbols, H_{symb}, is significant at the 1% level for all text samples.

2/11. Table of narrowed boundaries of the subjective information of non-letter symbols

Old boundary values (bits per branching point)			New boundary values (bits per branching point)			$\Delta = \hat{H}_{mean} - H_{mean}$
$\hat{H}_{min}$	$\hat{H}_{max}$	$\hat{H}_{mean}$	H_{min}	H_{max}	H_{mean}	
0.12	0.32	0.22	0.25	0.29	0.27	−0.05
0.16	0.40	0.28	0.28	0.32	0.30	−0.02
0.18	0.43	0.31	0.33	0.36	0.345	−0.035
0.19	0.45	0.32	0.36	0.39	0.375	−0.055
0.21	0.48	0.35	0.30	0.35	0.325	0.025
0.22	0.50	0.36	0.36	0.39	0.375	−0.015
0.26	0.56	0.41	0.36	0.41	0.385	0.025
0.27	0.57	0.42	0.37	0.42	0.395	0.025
0.28	0.58	0.43	0.34	0.43	0.375	0.055
0.28	0.58	0.43	0.44	0.49	0.465	−0.035
0.31	0.62	0.47	0.43	0.49	0.46	0.01
0.32	0.63	0.48	0.46	0.52	0.49	−0.01
0.33	0.65	0.49	0.50	0.55	0.465	0.025
0.35	0.67	0.51	0.54	0.61	0.575	−0.065
0.36	0.68	0.52	0.45	0.48	0.465	0.055
0.37	0.69	0.53	0.60	0.65	0.625	−0.095
0.38	0.70	0.54	0.50	0.55	0.525	0.015
0.41	0.73	0.57	0.49	0.57	0.53	0.04
0.41	0.73	0.57	0.58	0.59	0.585	−0.015
0.48	0.80	0.64	0.69	0.75	0.72	−0.08

Text: See note 2/10 arithmetic book, chemistry book, business notes. Pooled information values for two subjects; data represent information per branching point.

2/12. Küpfmüller (1954) describes the same experimental technique:
"A coherent text is masked following an arbitrarily determined word. The preceding text is read and an attempt is made to supply the next word from this text and its coherence. For a large number of such experiments, the number of correct guesses relative to the total number of attempts will yield a measure of the connections between words and sentences. It is shown that for one and the same text, for instance novels, scientific writing etc., from one and the same author, a constant final value is fairly rapidly obtained for the ratio of correct guesses to all guesses (from 100 to 200 guesses upwards). But this ratio depends fairly strongly upon the kind of text. Values between 15 and 33 % are obtained for different sorts of texts, the average being 22 %. Thus about 22 % of the words on average may be supplied from the coherence. In other words, the number of words in a long text may be reduced by a factor of 0.78 without detracting from its communication content. Then by definition the entropy becomes

$$0.78 \cdot 2.0 = 1.56 \; CU/ltr"$$

where CU equals bits and stands for Communication Units.
Küpfmüller then applied the same procedure to syllables and found that on average 46 % of the syllables could be predicted. Here Küpfmüller observed there was already a very strong dependence of the number of correct guesses on the particular text used. However, he did not go on to explore the question of text dependence; he simply worked out an average value on which he based his subsequent reasoning.

2/13. Table. Subjective information of small and capital letters

text	Number of signs			[bits/symbol]									
	text	sample word	starts	exptl. groups			control group						
				H (S/C)	$H(C)$	H S, C)	H(S)	$T(C,S)$	$\sigma_M(T)$	ΔH	$\sigma_M(\Delta H)$	N	
A	6315	2793	383	1.62	0.09	1.71	1.64	0.02	0.083	0.07	0.082	8	
B	6266	2091	287	1.66	0.07	1.73	1.71	0.05	0.126	0.02	0.132	6	
C	5901	1947	288	1.16	0.06	1.22	1.17	0.01	0.062	0.05	0.066	6	
D	6709	1546	192	1.62	0.08	1.70	1.64	0.02	0.099	0.06	0.102	12	
E	6197	1473	192	1.47	0.06	1.54	1.47	0	0.058	0.07	0.065	12	
F	3425	1627	246	1.55	0.12	1.67	1.65	0.10	0.052	0.02	0.061	20	
total	34813	11477	1588	1.51	0.09	1.60	1.55	0.04	0.033	0.05	0.035	64	

H (S):   subjective information of text (signs).
H (C):   subjective information of digital decision about capitals or small initial letters (capitals).
H (S/C): conditional subjective information of text when words are known to start with capital or small letters.
$H(C, S) = H(C) + H(S/C)$: Total information when capital and small letters are used.
$T(C, S) = H(S) - H(S/C)$: Transinformation of H (C) onto H (S).
$H = H(C, S) - H(S)$:   Information of capital and small letter usage.
N = number of subjects in experimental group (= N (control group))

List of texts:
    A. Physics book: R. W. Pohl, Vol. I Mechanik, Akustik u. Wärmelehre, 13th ed., Berlin 1955, section 74, pp 114-6, abridged.
    B. Newspaper text: "Rheinischer Merkur", 24 November 1967, leading article: "Streik gegen den Staat", abridged.
    C. Teaching program text, Weltner/Zorn, "Physikalische Kräfte und ihre Messung", experimental version, frames 1–28.
    D. Magazine text, "Der Spiegel", 23/1967, "Zukunft mit Zwittern", p. 146, abridged.
    E. Magazine text, "Umschau in Wissenschaft und Technik", 1961, no. 23, Hertel, "VTOL: Schnelle Verkehrsflugzeuge, die senkrecht starten und landen", p. 729; rephrased and abridged.
    F. Advertisement texts.
T (C. S) and H could not be shown to be significant at the 1 % level for any text.

3/1. At present only very incomplete statements may be made about the realization of such models, since neither neurophysiologists nor psychologists are currently able to state with certainty the structure of the neuronal networks which could explain how man's brain functions. Nevertheless, the existence of internal models of the external world is proved by the transinformation of these models onto perception fields and messages. For the time being all we can say about such models is that they reproduce certain object domains of the external world isomorphously or partly so. A model, B, will be isomorphous with respect to a number of objects, O, if the model contains b_j elements clearly associated with o_j elements of the set of objects. Further, the connections between the elements b_j must also be reproductions of the connections between the elements o_j of the object domain. What is said here about internal models was stated lucidly by Heinrich Hertz (1894) with reference to physics. He said that the statements made by physicists concerning natural phenomena were in the nature of a system of symbols isomorphous to these phenomena:

"We construct internal pictures or symbols of external objects of such a kind that the necessary sequences of thought images are always images of the necessary sequences in nature of the objects reproduced. For such requirements to be met at all, there must be a set of agreements between nature and our minds. Experience teaches us that this requirement is in fact met and hence that such agreements do exist". See also Chapter 4.

3/2a. In our example of a physics lesson, too, transinformation analysis might have been carried out by guessing-game methods. If applied often enough to the situation of the unknown circuit, such experiments would have given the probability of a correct answer of $p_j = \frac{1}{4}$ with $H_0 = 2$ bits so long as four alternative answers were available. After the message imparted by the teacher, this probability would have increased to $\frac{1}{3}$. With a large enough number of trials this figure would also have been obtained empirically, as would $H_1 = 1.58$ also. Here too, the difference would have been the transinformation of the teacher's message onto the event field. Finally, once the measurement has been made, no further guessing is required at all, provided the relationship is known, and thus the transinformation of the measurement would also have been empirically determined by means of the guessing game. However, if the relationship is not known, the probability of a correct answer remains $\frac{1}{3}$; from this we may conclude that transinformation of the internal model onto the product field, i.e. knowledge, is lacking. This also happens in examinations where the uncertainty regarding a product field is determined, the uncertainty of this product field being zero when the relationships are known. If only some of the examination questions relate to the knowledge to be tested, the transinformation of this knowledge onto the field of the examination questions is less than its information. Conversely, the transinformation of the examination answers onto the internal model also is smaller. When the questions are poorly formulated, the examiner learns little, or only something irrelevant, about the knowledge he is testing.

3/2b. An early method for the analysis of the information of product fields was provided by Garner and Hake (1951) in the form of a multivariate information analysis; see also Attneave (1965). In multivariate analysis, the transinformation is determined for so-called absolute judgments with respect to certain variable stimuli. These stimuli may be loudness of noises, size of geometric figures, interpolated values in scale readings, pitch of sounds, etc. The experimental set-up must always allow for:

1. classification of the stimuli offered
2. classification of the associated judgments.

The information of both fields and also of the product field can then be calculated directly. Information analysis can also be extended to problems with more than two fields.

3/3. The concept of aesthetic information is here defined in a different sense from the one in which it is commonly used. Aesthetic information is a measure of the degrees of freedom in the formulation of a text in which the semantic information is constant. Aesthetic information is not a measure of the "elegance" of the formulation. Within the restricted field of use of methods derived from information theory for educational purposes, the concept of aesthetic information is unlikely to lead to misunderstandings. Marko (1967) called aesthetic information "free entropy". Sometimes, in the literature of information theory, aesthetic information is called syntactic information, as opposed to semantic information. All three synonymous concepts are liable to misunderstanding. The aesthetic information of a message is that information which is not semantic information and not pragmatic information.

3/4. In developing teaching programs, one assumes that the teaching material holds didactic information for the user. If this assumption is incorrect, the flow of didactic information falls to zero when the teaching program is worked. If the "expert" learns nothing on working through the teaching program, he is simply absorbing its aesthetic information. This cannot as a rule fully occupy his perception capacity, so that the text appears to him highly redundant and banal. The disappearance of the didactic information of teaching program texts for experts is one reason why such experts systematically underestimate the level of difficulty of teaching programs for the user. This underestimation is inevitable because, for the user, the didactic information rate does not approach zero.

3/5 Table. Didactic information and didactic transinformation of a teaching program
for children in Volksschulen and Realschulen

	Realschule						Volksschule			
	grade						grade			
	5	6	7	8	9	10	6	7	8	9
H_{sub}(bit/S) before program (BP)	2.03	1.72	1.51	1.20	1.20	1.10	2.32	1.75	1.90	1.98
H_{sub}(bit/S) after program (AP)	1.48	1.08	1.07	0.92	0.97	0.91	1.65	1.25	1.56	1.51
didactic information (bit/S)	1.10	0.79	0.58	0.27	0.27	0.17	1.39	0.82	0.97	1.05
didactic transinform. (bit/S)	0.55	0.64	0.44	0.28	0.23	0.19	0.67	0.50	0.34	0.47
didactic information (bits)	5550	3990	2930	1360	1360	860	7020	4140	4900	5300
didactic transinformation (bits)	2780	3240	2480	1410	1160	960	3380	2520	1720	2380
average study time (minutes)	150	140	135	110	115	95	165	150	150	135
information flow (bits/second)	0.31	0.39	0.31	0.21	0.17	0.17	0.34	0.28	0.19	0.30

Teaching program: Weltner/Kunze: Der Viertaktmotor; experimental version. Basic text: 5050 signs. Total sample: 1119 signs. Sample per subject: 12 words (95 ± 10 signs). Subjects per class: 12

Variance Analysis: Overall Result

Variation	Sum of square	df	mean squares	F
Schools	7.60	1	7.60	47
BP, AP	5.55	1	5.55	38
Classes	1.87	3	0.62	3.88
Schools × (BP, AP)	0.18	1	0.18	1.1
Schools × classes	1.02	3	0.34	2.13
(BP, AP) × classes	0.53	3	0.18	1.1
(BP, AP) × classes × schools	0.07	3	0.023	–
within	28.42	176	0.161	
Total	45.24	191		

3/6. Table. Didactic information and didactic transinformation of a teaching program;
older schoolchildren and students

	N_{subj}	H_{sub} (bit/S)		bit/S		bits		Est. average working time	Inf. flow (bit /sec)
		BP	AP	did. inf.	trans. inf.	did. inf.	trans. inf.		
Univ. students	18	1.52	0.96	0.59	0.56	885	840	40	0.35
Tech. coll. students	24	1.42	0.93	0.59	0.59	885	885	40	0.37
Older school- children	24	1.99	0.98	1.06	1.01	1590	1520	50	0.51
Older school- children	30	1.86	0.85	0.93	1.01	1400	1520	50	0.51
Engng. students	24	1.67	0.94	0.74	0.73	1110	1100	50	0.37

Teaching program: Grundlagen der Datenverarbeitung Heft 3: "Flip Flop, Schieberegister", Ed.: Telefunken Basic text: 1500 signs

3/7. Table. Semantic and aesthetic transinformation of different texts during the reading process

Text	A_1	B_1	A_2	B_2	A_3	B_3	A_4	B_4	average value
N_{subj}	24	24	21	21	24	24	24	24	
no. of signs	5480	3990	6300	5700	6900	6500	5900	5700	
total sample text	1250	1100	2130	1890	1530	1440	2200	2100	
a: H_{sub}	1.70	1.49	1.64	1.34	1.72	1.55	1.68	1.69	
$\sigma_M(a)$	0.12	0.14	0.10	0.07	0.09	0.07	0.12	0.09	
b: H_{sub}	1.56	1.27	1.60	1.45	1.74	1.51	1.48	1.40	
$\sigma_M(b)$	0.14	0.12	0.09	0.10	0.07	0.06	0.07	0.08	
(bit/S) c: H_{sub}	1.38	1.06	1.51	1.17	1.43	1.36	–	–	
$\sigma_M(c)$	0.14	0.10	0.08	0.09	0.13	0.06	–	–	
T_{sem}	0.14	0.22	0.04	−0.11	−0.02	0.04	0.20	0.29	0.10
T_{aesth}	0.18	0.21	0.09	0.28	0.31	0.15	–	–	0.20
$T_{sem\ \&\ aesth}$	0.32	0.43	0.13	0.17	0.29	0.19	–	–	0.26
T^*_{sem}	765	880	252	− 626	− 138	260	1180	1160	466
(bit) T^*_{aesth}	985	840	567	1596	2138	975	–	–	1183
$T^*_{sem\ \&\ aesth}$	1750	1720	819	970	2000	1235	–	–	1416
(min) t	5.5	4.2	5.8	5.8	5.6	5.6	30	30	
c_{sem}	2.3	3.5	0.7	–	–	0.8	0.7	0.9	1.5
(bit/sec) $c_{aesth.}$	3.0	3.3	1.6	4.6	6.3	2.9	–	–	3.6
$c_{sem\ \&\ aesth}$	5.3	6.8	2.3	2.8	5.9	3.7	–	–	4.5

a: read neither text; b: read other text; c: read own text; σ_M: sample error; T_{sem}: semantic transinformation; T_{aesth}: aesthetic transinformation; $T_{sem\ \&\ aesth}$: semantic and aesthetic transinformation t: average reading (processing) time; c: information flow.

Bibliography

A_1: "Bombe am Bauch", Spiegel, 6 June 1966.
B_1: rewritten, simplified text of same content as A_1.
B_2: "Meerwasser-Entsalzung", Spiegel, 33/1961, abridged.
A_3: "Zukunft mit Zwittern", Spiegel, 23/1961, abridged.
B_3: Hertel, "VTOL: Schnelle Verkehrsflugzeuge, die senkrecht starten und landen", Umschau in Wissenschaft und Technik, 1961, Heft 23, rewritten and abridged.
A_4: "Riesen am Rande", Spiegel, 3/1964, abridged.
B_4: Rudolph, "Neu entdeckte Radioquellen an den Grenzen der Sichtbarkeit", Umschau in Wissenschaft und Technik, 1964, Heft 5, restructured and abridged.

3/8. Table. Memory test. Text: E. Kästner: "Nordafrikanische Wüste". No. of signs S = 1852.

No. of subjects	N = 8		
	(bit/S)		
	H_{sub}	σ_M	Transinf. T
First reading	2.42	0.13	–
after 20 minutes	1.36	0.12	1.06
after 4 days	1.78	0.10	0.64
after 8 days	2.06	0.13	0.34

3/9. Jarvik (1951) used a similar procedure to investigate the learning of probability (informational accommodation). In his scheme, sequences of 2 or 4 symbols are given to the subjects in advance; these symbols are defined only with respect to their frequency distribution but do not obey definite rules. Sequences are then presented to the subjects who are asked to continue them. It is found that the subjects in their continuation of the probability distribution adopt the given sequence. When the frequency distribution is changed. the subjects consciously or unconsciously carry out similar changes; see Frank (1960). The learning of probability from stochastic sign sequences does not depend upon intelligence. Even after the learning process is complete, the subjective information of stochastic sign sequences can never approach zero.

4/1. Itelson provides nine possible learning models in his diagram:

external world	Learning system		
	deterministic automaton (a_D)	Probability automata (a_p)	
		Markov automaton a_M)	automaton with random reactions (a_s)
deterministic automaton (a_D)	$a_D a_D$	$a_D a_M$ (example: A. A. Liapunov's model)	$a_D a_s$ (example: Bush-Mosteller model)
Markov automaton (a_M)	$a_M a_D$ (example: W. R. Ashby's model)	$a_M a_M$ (example: Miller's model)	$a_M a_s$ (example: Estes' model)
automaton with random reactions a_S)	$a_S a_D$ (example: M. L. Zetlin's model)	$a_S a_M$ (example: industrial regulators)	$a_S a_S$ (example: Ashby's homeostat)

4/2. Educational theorists have always objected to the educational values of science and technology because they claimed that the preoccupation with technical subject matter meant that only isolated facts were learned. The resulting inadequate knowledge of science and technology gave rise to a deplorable and mistaken assessment of these disciplines, particularly among German-speaking teachers. Basically this involves a confusion between result and process. Anyone who regards science or technology as a closed collection of results or constructions, thus merely as the elements of a field, will reach a different conclusion about the educational value of these disciplines from anyone who sees them as ongoing processes of scientific research or technological change in the environment, thus as the transinformation of the operators. Whereas a passive acceptance of facts and results would indeed have only a slight transinformation onto the external world, this is certainly not true of the processes and methods of science and technology.

This fact emerges particularly clearly from the development of models in cybernetics. Such models have a high transinformation onto many object domains in our scientific, technological, social, and educational external world. This is apparent from the fact that authors whose work is far removed from cybernetics and computer science do in fact use cybernetic thought models: see H. v. Hentig: Die Schule im Regelkreis.

4/3. With the following symbols:
H_0 = information of the product field before the learning process;
H_1 = information of the product field after the learning process.
one obtains the relationships below for these concepts:
a) Itelson: $H_1 = H_0 - K$,
where the informedness K is a measure of knowledge.

b) Von Cube calls it redundancy:

$$R = \frac{H_0 - H_1}{H_0}$$

We call it transinformation of knowledge onto the product field:

$$T = H_0 - H_1$$

These relations are formally interchangeable. In particular, K and T are numerically identical.

Literature

1. Adelson, M., Muckler, F. A., Williams, A. C.: Verbal learning and message variables related to amount of information. In: Quastler, H.: Information Theory in Psychology, p. 291–299, Illinois, 1955.
2. Amthauer, R.: Intelligenz und Beruf. Ergebnisse eines neuen Verfahrens zur Bestimmung der Intelligenz. Zeitschr. f. exp. und angew. Psych. 1, p. 102–136 (1953).
3. Anschütz, H.: Die Verteilung der Begriffe in Lehrprogrammtexten. In: H. Frank (Ed.): Lehrmaschinen in kybernetischer und pädagogischer Sicht, Vol. 3. Stuttgart 1965.
4. Atkinson, R. C., Paulson, J. A.: An Approach to the Psychology of Instruction. In: Psychological Bulletin, 1972.
5. Attneave, F.: Psychology probability as a function of experienced frequency. J. exp. Psych. 46, p. 81–86 (1953).
6. Attneave, F.: Some informational aspects of visual perception. Psych. Rev. 61, p. 183–193 (1954).
7. Attneave, F.: Symmetry, information and memory for patterns. Amer. J. Psych. 68, p. 209–222 (1955).
8. Attneave, F.: Applications of Information Theory to Psychology. A summary of basic concepts, methods and results. New York 1959.
9. Bennet, W. F., Fitts, P. M., Noble, M.: The Learning of Sequential Dependencies. Journ. exp. Psych. 48, p. 303–312 (1954).
10. Bartlett, C.: Remembering, a study in experimental and social psychology. Cambridge: University Oven 1932.
11. Bloom, B. S. (Ed.): Taxonomy of educational objectives. The classification of educational goals. Handbook I: Cognitive Domain. New York 1956.
12. Bongard, M. M.: Über den Begriff der nützlichen Information. In: Ljapunow (Ed.): Probleme der Kybernetik. p. 91–104, Berlin 1966.
13. Bung, K.: A theoretical model for programmed language instruction. Ph. D.-Dissertation. Cambridge: Cambridge University, Great Britain, 1972.
14. Bürmann, G., Frank, H., Lorenz, L.: Informationstheoretische Untersuchungen über Rang und Länge deutscher Wörter. GrKG 4, p. 73–90 (1963).
15. Burton, N. G., Licklider, J. C. R.: Longrange constraints in the statistical structure of printed English. Amer. J. Psych. 68, 4, p. 650–653 (1955).
16. Carson, D. H.: Letter constraints within words in printed English. Kybernetik I, 46, p. 46–54 (1961).
17. Charkewitsch, A. A.: Über den Wert einer Information. In: Ljapunow (Ed.): Probleme der Kybernetik. Berlin 1964.
18. Cherry, C.: Kommunikationsforschung — eine neue Wissenschaft. Stuttgart 1963.
19. Chintschin, A. J.: Über grundlegende Sätze der Informationstheorie. In: Grell, H. (Ed.): Arbeiten zur Informationstheorie I. Berlin 1957.
20. Correll, W.: Programmiertes Lernen und schöpferisches Denken. München, Basel 1965.
21. Cube von, F.: Grundsätzliche Probleme bei der Anwendung der Shannonschen Formel auf Wahrnehmungstheorie und Lerntheorie. GrKG 1, p. 17–24 (1960a).
22. Cube von, F.: Über informationstheoretische Probleme in Lerntheorie und Didaktik. GrKG 1, p. 105–112 (1960b).

23. Cube von, F.: Über ein Verfahren der mechanischen Didaktik. GrKG **2**, p. 7–10 (1961).
24. Cube von, F.: Entwurf eines Lernmodells auf der Basis der Informationstheorie. GrKG **3**, p. 57–63 (1962).
25. Cube von, F.: Informationstheoretische Untersuchungen zum Problem des Auswendig-lernens. In: Zeitschrift für exp. und angew. Psych. **10** (1963).
26. Cube von, F.: Kybernetische Grundlagen des Lernens und Lehrens. Stuttgart, 1965[1], 1968[2].
27. Czemper, K.- A., Boswau, H.: Unterricht und Computer, München 1965.
28. Eckel, K.: Vorschläge zur Definition empirischer Lernbegriffe. In: Lehrmaschinen in kybernetischer und pädagogischer Sicht, Vol. 4, Stuttgart, München 1966.
29. Englert, L., Frank, H., Schiefele, H., Stachowiak, H.: Lexikon der kybernetischen Pädagogik und der Programmierten Instruktion. Quickborn 1966.
30. Eriksen, C. W., Hake, H. W.: Absolute judgements as a function of the stimulus range and the number of stimulus and response categories. USAF: WADC Technical Report, p. 54–162 (1954).
31. Estes, W. K.: Toward a statistical theory of learning. Psych. Rev. **57**, p. 94–107 (1950).
32. Estoup, J. B.: Gammes sténographiques. Paris, 1916, 4. Aufl., zitiert nach Mandelbrot, 1957.
33. Fischer, H.: Koordination von Unterrichtsthemen. In: Rollett, B., Weltner, K. (Ed.): Fortschritte und Ergebnisse der Bildungstechnologie II. München 1973.
34. Flechsig, K.-H.: Erziehen zur Kreativität. Neue Sammlung 6, H. 2, Göttingen 1966.
35. Flechtner, H. J.: Grundbegriffe der Kybernetik. Stuttgart 1967[2].
36. Foerster von, H.: Self Organising Systems and their Environments. In: Self Organising Systems. Ed. by Yovitts, M. C., Cameron, S. Pergamon 1960.
37. Foppa, K.: Lernen, Gedächtnis, Verhalten. Köln 1966[2].
38. Frank, H.: Über eine informationspsychologische Maßbestimmung der semantischen und pragmatischen Information. GrKG **1**, p. 25–32 (1960a).
39. Frank, H.: Über die Kapazitäten der menschlichen Sinnesorgane. GrKG **1**, p. 145–152 (1960b).
40. Frank, H.: Über das Intelligenzproblem in der Informationspsychologie. GrKG **1**, p. 85–96 (1960c).
41. Frank, H.: Zum Problem des vorbewußten Gedächtnisses. GrKG **2**, p. 17–24 (1961).
42. Frank, H., Klugmann, D., Wendt, S.: Über den Informationsgehalt der deutschen Sprache. GrKG **4**, p. 65–72 (1963).
43. Frank, H.: Kybernetische Analysen subjektiver Sachverhalte. Quickborn 1964a.
44. Frank, H.: Über den nicht-negativen Erwartungswert von $i_{sub}(z_i) - i(z_j)$. GrKG **5**, p. 25–30 (1964b).
45. Frank, H.: Informationswissenschaftliche Gesetze in der natürlichen deutschen Sprache. In: Frank, H. (Ed.): Kybernetik — Brücke zwischen den Wissenschaften. Frankfurt 1969, 7. Auflage.
46. Frank, H.: Zur kybernetisch-pädagogischen Theorie der Skinner-Algorithmen. GrKG **6**, (1965b).
47. Frank, H.: Ansätze zum algorithmischen Lehralgorithmieren. In: Frank, H. (Ed.): Lehrmaschinen in kybernetischer und pädagogischer Sicht, Vol. 4, p. 70–112, Stuttgart, München 1966.
48. Frank, H.: Über den Informationsgehalt von Bildern. GrKG **8**, p. 23–31 (1967).
49. Frank, H., Frank-Böhringer, B.: Begriff und Funktion der ästhetischen Information in Lehrprogrammen. In: Praxis und Perspektiven des programmierten Unterrichts, Band II, p. 32–36, Quickborn 1967.
50. Frank, H., Graf, K.-D.: Über eine formale Didaktik. In: Praxis und Perspektiven des programmierten Unterrichts, Vol.II, p. 87–91, Quickborn 1967.
51. Frank, H.: Kybernetische Grundlagen der Pädagogik. Baden-Baden 1962. 2nd Edition 1969.

52. Frick, F. C., Sumby, W. H.: Control tower language. Acoust Soc. Amer. **24**, p. 595–596 (1952).
53. Fucks, W.: Nach allen Regeln der Kunst. Stuttgart 1969.
54. Gardner, R. A.: Probability-learning with two and three choices. Amer. J. Psych. **70**, p. 174–185 (1957).
55. Gray, W. S.: Summary of investigations relating to reading. Chicago 1925.
56. Gray, W. S.: The Teaching of Reading and Writing: An International Survey. Monographs on Fundamental Education, 1956a.
57. Gray, W. S., Rogers, B.: Maturity in Reading: Its Nature and Appraisal. Chicago 1956b.
58. Griew, S.: Information transmission and age. In: Williams, R. H. (Ed.): Process of aging, p. 63–79, New York 1963.
59. Groeben, N.: Die Verständlichkeit von Unterrichtstexten. In: Arbeiten zur sozialwissenschaftlichen Psychologie. Münster 1971.
60. Hake, H. W., Garner, W. R.: The effect of presenting various numbers of discrete steps on scale reading accuracy. J. of exp. Psych. **42**, p. 358–366 (1951).
61. Hansson, H.: The entropy of the Swedish language. Proc. of the 2nd Prague Symposium on Information Theory. Prague 1960.
62. Heimann, P.: Didaktik als Theorie und Lehre. Die deutsche Schule 1962/9.
63. Heinrich, P.-B.: Durchführung von Rateversuchen mit Hilfe eines Rechners. GrKG Vol. **11** (1970).
64. Hentig, H. V.: Die Schule im Regelkreis. Stuttgart 1966.
65. Herrmann, Th.: Informationstheoretische Modelle zur Darstellung der kognitiven Ordnung. In: Bergius (Ed.): Handbuch der Psychologie, Bd. I/2, p. 641–669. Göttingen 1964.
66. Herdan, G.: The advanced theory of language as choice and chance. Berlin, Heidelberg, New York 1966.
67. Hertz, H.: Drei Bilder der Mechanik (1894). In: Physikalische Blätter, 13. Jg., Mosbach (Baden) 1957.
68. Heß, H.: Zur Psychologie des Gedächtnisses IV. Determination und Behalten sinnvollen sprachlichen Materials bei Berücksichtigung von gestörtem Kontext. Zeitschrift für Psychologie **80**, 3–4, p. 151–170 (1965).
69. Hick, W. E.: On the rate of gain of information. Quart. J. exp. Psych. **4**, p. 11–26 (1952).
70. Hilgard, E. R.: Theories of Learning. 2nd Ed. 1956.
71. Hochheimer, W.: Bemerkungen und Fragen zu den psychologischen Grundlagen von Pädotechnologie und Lehrprogrammen. In: Zeitschrift für Erziehungswissenschaftliche Forschung, Heft 1, 1967.
72. Hofstätter, P. R.: Über Ähnlichkeit. Psyche **9**, p. 54–80 (1955).
73. Hörmann, H.: Psychologie der Sprache. Berlin, Heidelberg 1967.
74. Huey, E. B.: The Psychology and pedagogy of Reading. Macmillan 1912.
75. Hyman, R.: Stimulus Information as a Determinant of Reaction Time. J. exp. Psych. **45**, p. 188–196 (1953).
76. Huffmann, D. A.: A method for the construction of minimum-redundancy codes. Proc. IRE, **40**, 9 (1952).
77. Itelson, L.: Mathematische und kybernetische Methoden in der Pädagogik. Berlin 1967.
78. Jaglom, A. M., Jaglom, I. M.: Wahrscheinlichkeit und Information. Berlin 1967.
79. Jarvik, M. E.: Probability learning and a negative recency effect in the serial anticipation of alternative symbols. J. exp. Psych. **41**, p. 291–297 (1951).
80. Judd, C. H.: The Relation of special Training to general Intelligence. Educ. Rev. 1908, R. 36.
81. Kaeding, F.-W.: Häufigkeitswörterbuch der deutschen Sprache. Steglitz bei Berlin 1897.

82. Kelbert, H.: Kybernetisches Modell der Abarbeitung eines programmierten ver-
    zweigten Lehrbuches 1. In: Frank, H. (Ed.): Lehrmaschinen in kyb. und päd. Sicht,
    Bd. 2. 1964.

83. Kerschensteiner, G.: Wesen und Wert des naturwissenschaftlichen Unterrichts. 4.
    Aufl., München 1952 (1st Edition 1914).

84. Klafki, W.: Das pädagogische Problem des Elementaren und die Theorie der kategoria-
    len Bildung. Weinheim, Berlin 1963.

85. Klafki, W.: Studien zur Bildungstheorie und Didaktik. 9. Edition. Weinheim 1967.

86. Klemmer, E. T., Frick, F. C.: Assimilation of information from dot and matrix patterns.
    J. exp. Psych. **45**, p. 15–19 (1953).

87. Klix, F.: Psychophysik kognitiver Prozesse. In: Marko (Ed.): Kybernetik **68**,
    München 1968.

88. Knöchel, W.: Grundlagenprobleme der Pädagogik in kybernetischer Sicht. Berlin
    1966.

89. Krah, W., Kirchberg, P., Schmädicke, I.: Zum Problem der Konzentrierbarkeit von
    Texten, Redundanzuntersuchungen an deutschen Texten. Zeitschrift für Phonetik,
    Sprachwissenschaft und Kommunikationsforschung. Vol. **18,** p. 85–94 (1965).

90. Küpfmüller, K.: Informationsverarbeitung durch den Menschen. Nachrichtentech-
    nische Zeitschrift, Vol. **12,** Nr. 2, p. 68–74 (1959).

91. Küpfmüller, K.: Die Entropie der deutschen Sprache. Fernmeldetechnische Zeit-
    schrift **7**, p. 265–271 (1954).

92. Kullback, S.: Informationtheory and statistics. New York, London 1959.

93. Landa, L. N.: Ein Versuch, die mathematische Logik und die Informationstheorie auf
    einige Probleme des Unterrichts anzuwenden. In: Kybernetische Probleme in Pädagogik
    und Psychologie. Psychologische Beiträge II, Nr. 3, Berlin 1963.

94. Landa, L. N.: Das Verhältnis zwischen heuristischen und algorithmischen Prozessen
    und einige Probleme ihrer Herausbildung durch den programmierten Unterricht. In:
    Wissenschaftliche Zeitschrift des Pädagogischen Instituts Güstrow, 5. Jg., p. 21–34
    (1966/67).

95. Langer, D.: Informationstheorie und Psychologie. Göttingen 1962.

96. Lánský, M.: Eine Bemerkung zum Begriff der Makrostruktur eines Lehralgorithmus.
    In: H. Frank (Ed.): Lehrmaschinen in kybernetischer und pädagogischer Sicht, Vol. 4.
    Stuttgart, München 1966.

97. Lánský, M.: Über ein Gruppierungsverfahren. In: Praxis und Perspektiven des pro-
    grammierten Unterrichts, Vol. II, Referate des V. Symposions über Lehrmaschinen,
    p. 103–104, Quickborn 1967.

98. Lánský, M.: Entwurf eines Algorithmus zur Bestimmung der optimalen Verteilung
    von Explanationen im Lehrprogramm. In: Rollett, B., Weltner, K. (Eds.): Perspektiven
    des programmierten Unterrichts. Wien 1970.

99. Laszlo, E.: An Introduction to System Philosophy. New York 1972.

100. MacKay, D. M.: In Search of Basic Symbols. Cybernetics. New York 1951

101. Mandelbrot, B.: Linguistique statistique macroscopique I (1957). In: J. Piaget (Ed.):
    Logique, Language et Théorie de L'information. Presses Universitaires de France. Paris
    1957.

102. Marko, H. (Ed.): Die Anwendung nachrichtentechnischer Methoden in der Biologie.
    Kybernetik **68**. München 1968.

103. Meier, H.: Deutsche Sprachstatistik. Vol. 1, Vol. 2. Hildesheim 1964.

104. Meili, R.: Gestaltprozesse und psychische Organisation. Beiheft z. Schweiz. Zeit-
    schrift f. Psychologie und ihre Anwendungen. 1954.

105. Meyer, G.: Kybernetik und Unterrichtsprozeß. Berlin 1966.

106. Meyer-Eppler, W.: Grundlagen und Anwendungen der Informationstheorie. Heidel-
    berg 1959 (2nd Ed. 1969).

107. Miller, G. A., Selfridge, J. A.: Verbal Context and the Recall of Meaningful Material. Amer. J. Psych. **63**, p. 176–185 (1950).

108. Miller, G. A., Bruner, J. S., Postman, L.: Familiarity of letter sequences and tachistoscopic identification. Journal of gen. Psychology Vol. **50**, p. 129–139 (1954).

109. Miller, G. A.: The magical number seven plus or minus two. Some limits on capacity for processing information. In: Reading in perception. New York-Toronto-London 1958.

110. Möller, B., Ch.: Perspektiven der didaktischen Forschung. München, Basel 1966.

111. Müller, D. D.: Bibliographie: Kybernetische Pädagogik, Programmierter Unterricht, Grenzgebiete. Berlin 1968.

112. Neidhardt, P.: Der Begriff des Wirkungsgrades in der Informationstheorie. In: Elektronische Rundschau **10**, p. 15–19 (1956).

113. Newman, E. B., Gerstman, L. S.: A new method for analyzing printed English. J. exp. Psych. **44**, p. 114–125 (1952).

114. Newman, E. B.: Men and information: a psychologist's view. Nuovo Cimento Suppl. **13**, p. 539–559 (1959).

115. Newman, E. B., Waugh, N. C.: The redundancy of texts in three languages. Information and Control **3**, p. 141–153 (1960).

116. Osgood, C. E.: The nature and measurement of meaning. Psych. Bull **49**, p. 197–237 (1952).

117. Pask, G. (1959): Adaptive Teaching with Adaptive Machines. In: Lumsdaine, A, A., Glaser, R. (Eds.): Teaching Machines and Programmed Learning, p. 349–366, Washington 1960.

118. Pask, G.: Anpassungsfähige Lehrmaschinen z. Gruppenschulung. pl. 3/1964.

119. Pask, G.: A Cybernetic Experimental Method and its Underlying Philosophy. In: Int. Journal of Man-Machine Studies **3**, p. 279–337 (1971).

120. Peters, J.: Einführung in die allgemeine Informationstheorie. Berlin, Heidelberg, New York 1966.

121. Piaget, J.: Psychologie der Intelligenz. 1966.

122. Pollack, I.: The assimilation of sequentially encoded information. Amer. J. Psych. **66** (1953).

123. Pollack, I., Ficks, L.: Information of multidimensional auditory displays. J. Acoust. Soc. Am. **26**, p. 155–158 (1954).

124. Postman, L.: Learned principles of organisation in memory. Psych. Monogr. **68**, 3, whole no. 374 (1954).

125. Quastler, H. (Ed.): Information Theory in Psychology. Illinois 1955.

126. Rauner, F., Krumme, W.: Erfahrungen bei der Anwendung der rechnerunabhängigen w-t-Didaktik mit Einschluß der Adressatenübungen an einem Modellrechner. In: Praxis und Perspektiven des Programmierten Unterrichts, Vol. 2, p. 81–68, Quickborn 1967.

127. Richter, H.: Wahrscheinlichkeitstheorie. Berlin, Göttingen, Heidelberg 1956.

128. Riedel, H.: Die Altersabhängigkeit informationspsychologischer Parameter und ihre mögliche Bedeutung für Lehralgorithmen. In: Frank, H. (Ed.): Lehrmaschinen in kybernetischer und pädagogischer Sicht, Vol.2. Stuttgart-München 1964.

129. Riedel, H.: Empirische Untersuchungen zur kybernetischen Pädagogik. Quickborn 1965.

130. Riedel, H.: Psychostruktur. Quickborn 1967a.

131. Riedel, H.: Empirische Untersuchung zu einem informationspsychologischen Gedächtnismodell. GrKG **8**, H. 1, p. 1–13 (1967b).

132. Rollett, B.: Untersuchungen zur semantischen Transinformation. In: Rollett, B., Weltner, K. (Eds.): Perspektiven des Programmierten Unterrichts. Wien 1970.

133. Rollett, B., Schick, A.: Some uses of informationtheory in itemanalysis of verbal intelligence tests: The Shannon-Weltner guessing-game. In: Rev. of Educ. Cybernetics and Applied Linguistics. London 1969.

134. Rollet, B.: Naturwissenschaften als "exakte Wissenschaften" — prädestiniert für die Lehrobjektivierung? In: Schmidt, H. (Ed.): Fachdidaktik und Lehrobjektivierung in den Naturwissenschaften, p. 28–33 (1972).

135. Roth, H.: Pädagogische Psychologie des Lehrens und Lernens. 1958.

136. Schmidt, A.: An experimental study in the psychology of reading. U Chicago, 1917.

137. Schmidt, H.: Denkschrift zur Gründung eines Institutes für Regeltechnik. 2nd Edition. Berlin 1941.

138. Schöler, W.: Entlastetes Lernen im Blickpunkt der Unterrichtsforschung. In: ZeF 1, p. 56–61 (1967a).

139. Schöler, W.: Über den Gegenstand der Unterrichtswissenschaft. In: ZeF I 4, p. 3–18 (1967b).

140. Shannon, C. E., Weaver, W.: The mathematical theory of communication. Bell System Tech. J. 27 (1948). University of Illinois Press, Urbana 1949, 1964.

141. Shannon, C. E.: Predication and entropy of printed English. Bell System Tech. 30, p. 50–64 (1951).

142. Shavelson, R. J.: Some Aspects of the Correspondence between Content Structure and Cognitive Structure in Physics Instruction. In: Journal of Educational Psychology 63, No. 3, p. 225–234 (1972).

143. Skinner, B. F. (1954): The science of learning and the art of teaching. In: Lumsdaine, A. A., Glaser, R. (Eds.): Teaching Machine and Programmed Learning, p. 99–113, Washington 1960.

144. Sprung, L.: Zur Psychologie des Gedächtnisses I. Über einige Abhängigkeitsbeziehungen zwischen Kontexteigenschaften und Reproduktionsleistungen in sinnvollen sprachlichen Texten. Z. f. Psych. 169, 1–2, p. 35–56 (1964).

145. Stachowiak, H.: Denken und Erkennen im kybernetischen Modell. Wien-New York 1965.

146. Stachowiak, H.: Zum Problem einer logisch-semantischen Maßbestimmung des Lernerfolgs. Beiheft zu Band 7 der GrKG (1966).

147. Steinbuch, K.: Bemerkungen zum Erkennen und Problemlösen. In: Marko (Ed.): Kybernetik 68. München 1968.

148. Steinbuch, K.: Automat und Mensch. Über menschliche und maschinelle Intelligenz. Heidelberg, 1st Edition 1961.

149. Stolurow, L. M.: Bildungstechnologie im Rahmen integrierter Curricula. In: Rollett, B., Weltner, K. (Eds.): Fortschritte und Ergebnisse der Bildungstechnologie II, München 1973.

150. Travers, R. M. W.: Informationsübertragung auf Menschen als Empfänger pl. 4/1966.

151. Thorndike, E. L.: Educational Psychology, Vol. II. The Psychology of Learning. New York 1914.

152. Vogt, H.: Programmierter Unterricht und Lehrmaschinen an Hoch- und Fachschulen der Sowjetunion. München 1965.

153. Wagenschein, M.: Die pädagogische Dimension der Physik. Braunschweig 1962.

154. Wertheimer, M.: Produktives Denken. Frankfurt 1957.

155. Weltner, K.: Gesichtspunkte zur Behandlung technischer Sachverhalte im Naturlehreunterricht. In: Die Deutsche Schule 12 (1963).

156. Weltner, K.: Eine vergleichende Untersuchung von Lernleistung und Erinnerungsfestigkeit bei programmiertem Unterricht und Direktunterricht. In: Frank, H. (Ed.): Lehrmaschinen in kybernetischer und pädagogischer Sicht, Vol. 2, p. 11–19, Stuttgart-München 1964a.

157. Weltner, K.: Zur empirischen Bestimmung subjektiver Informationswerte von Lehr-buchtexten mit dem Ratetest nach Shannon. GrKG, p. 3–11 (1964b).

158. Weltner, K.: Der Shannonsche Ratetest in der Praxis der Programmierten Instruktion. In: Frank, H. (Ed.): Lehrmaschinen in kybernetischer und pädagogischer Sicht, Vol. 4. Stuttgart-München 1966.

159. Weltner, K.: Subjektive Information von deutschen Texten und didaktische Trans-information. In: Bericht über den 25. Kongreß der Deutschen Gesellschaft für Psycho-logie, p. 294–301. Göttingen 1967a.

160. Weltner, K.: Zur Bestimmung der subjektiven Information durch Ratetests. In: Praxis und Perspektiven des Programmierten Unterrichts, Vol. 2, p. 69–74. Quickborn 1967b.

161. Weltner, K.: Informationspsychologische Ansätze in der Pädagogik. In: Kroebel, W. (Ed.): Fortschritte der Kybernetik, p. 299–321. München 1967c.

162. Weltner, K., Strunz, K.: Kybernetische Pädagogik. In: Strunz, K. (Ed.): Pädagogi-sche Psychologie für höhere Schulen, 4. Kapitel, p. 326–356. München 1967.

163. Weltner, K.: Informationspsychologie und programmierte Instruktion. In: Marko, Kybernetik 1968. München 1968.

164. Weltner, K., Kunze, W.: Der Viertaktmotor. Teaching Program. Stuttgart 1968.

165. Weltner, K.: Präzisierung der Bestimmung der subjektiven Information von Texten und Berücksichtigung gemischter Repertoires. In: Irle (Ed.): Bericht über den 26. Kongreß der Deutschen Gesellschaft für Psychologie. Göttingen 1969.

166. Weltner, K.: Zur Bestimmung der subjektiven Information. In: Rollett, B., Weltner, K. (Eds.): Perspektiven des Programmierten Unterrichts. Wien 1970.

167. Weltner, K., Heinrich, P. B.: Einsatz des Nixdorf-Rechners bei Untersuchungen zur Informationspsychologie. In: Rollett, B., Weltner, K. (Eds.): Perspektiven des Pro-grammierten Unterrichts. Wien 1970.

168. Weltner, K., Heinrich, P. B., Heinze, N.: Über den Zusammenhang der verschiedenen Verfahren zur Messung der subjektiven Information. In: Rollett, Weltner (Eds.): Fortschritte und Ergebnisse der Unterrichtstechnologie, p. 288–293. München 1971.

169. Wiener, N.: Cybernetics or Control and Communication in the Animal and the Machine. New York, Paris 1948.

170. Wittgenstein, L.: Tractus logico-Philosophicus. (Logisch-Philosophische Abhand-lung). Nachdruck aus den Analen der Naturphilosophie (1921) mit beigefügter englischer Übersetzung und einer Einführung von Bertrand Russell. London 1922 (5. Auflage 1951).

171. Woodworth, R., Schlossberg, H.: Experimental Psychology. New York 1954.

172. Zemanek, H.: Elementare Informationstheorie. Wien-München 1959.

173. Zemanek, H.: Lernende Automaten. In: Steinbuch, K. (Ed.): Taschenbuch der Nach-richtenverarbeitung. Berlin 1961.

174. Zipf, G. K.: Human Behavior and the Principle of Least Effort. Cambridge, Mass. 1949.

Author Index

Page numbers in *italics* refer to the Literature

Subject Index

Kommunikation und Kybernetik
in Einzeldarstellungen

Herausgegeben von H. Wolter und W. D. Keidel

Preisänderungen vorbehalten

Psycholinguistics

An Introduction to Research and Theory

By H. Hörmann, Ruhr-Universität Bochum
Translated from the German Edition by H. H. Stern

With 69 figures. XII, 377 pages. 1971
Cloth DM 68,—; US $27.90
ISBN 3-540-05159-7
Soft cover DM 39,50; US $16.20
ISBN 3-540-05665-3

A new, scholarly and systematic introduction to psycholinguistic thought and research, seen against the background of psychology, philosophy and linguistics, and based on a thorough and wideranging review of North American and European writings in this field.

Contents: Sign, Expression and Symbol. Linguistic Units. Language and Communication. The Probability Structure of Language. Phenomenology of Verbal Associations. The 'Mechanism' of Association. The Philosophical Background to Modern Psycholinguistics. The Field Concept of Meaning. Mediation Theories of Language Processes. The Conditioning Theory of Meaning. The Imitation of Sounds and Sound Symbolism. The Psychological Reality of Grammar. Genetic and Child Psychology as a Testing Ground for Psycholinguistics. The Influence of Language on Man's View of the World.

Zeichenerkennung durch biologische und technische Systeme
Pattern Recognition in Biological and Technical Systems

Tagungsbericht des 4. Kongresses der Deutschen Gesellschaft für Kybernetik, durchgeführt an der Technischen Universität Berlin vom 6.—9. April 1970
Proceedings of the 4th Congress of the Deutsche Gesellschaft für Kybernetik held at Berlin, Technical University, April 6—9, 1970

Edited by O.-J. Grüsser and R. Klinke, Freie Universität Berlin

Mit 182 Abbildungen. XII, 413 Seiten (22 Beiträge in Englisch,
14 Beiträge in Deutsch). 1971
Gebunden DM 89,—; US $36.50
ISBN 3-540-05385-9

Das Buch gibt einen Überblick über den gegenwärtigen Stand der Analyse zeichenerkennender Systeme bei Mensch und Tier, sowie über die Möglichkeiten, ähnliche Systeme technisch zu realisieren.

Inhaltsübersicht: Allgemeine Theorie der Zeichenerkennung — General Theory of Pattern Recognition. — Zeichenerkennung in biologischen und technischen Systemen — Pattern Recognition in Biological and Technical Systems.

Preisänderungen vorbehalten